The Road to Getting Yourself Out of the Way
A Journey to Effortless Living

Annette Birkmann

The Road to Getting Yourself Out of the Way
A Journey to Effortless Living

Copyright © 2012 Annette Birkmann
All Rights Reserved

Cover: Copyright © 2012 Mette Sophia Damgaard
Formatting: Greg Banks, BDDesign LLC

ISBN-13: 978-1-105-85168-1

www.annettebirkmann.com

*It is escape from "what is",
the endeavour to reach something other than
"what is", that creates conflict.*

J. Krishnamurti

ACKNOWLEDGMENTS

I would like to thank all the people who have supported me on this journey and those who have helped in various ways with the preparation of this book. In particular I would like to express my gratitude:

To my family for your support and complete trust in me and for never trying to talk me out of my motorcycle adventure; to Gitte Karen Rosenqvist for your support and ability to listen in calm presence; to Mariano Calderon who ceaselessly helped and supported me in Buenos Aires – thank you for always being there for me, without you I doubt this adventure would have happened; to Roberto Baum for invaluable support in Chile; to the Ibarra family in Formosa for helping me when stranded in the middle of nowhere; to Vicky Gómez Echeverri and Camilo Perez Gomez for showing me the true beauty of Colombia and its people; to Jens Rosendal, Arturo Figueroa, Luis Rangel and Jose Luis Salazar Lara for helping me through the accident in Mexico City – your support meant nothing less than the world to me; to Chris Dawe for your endless support, help and hospitality and for introducing me to riders across the United States, many of whom are now my dear friends; to Chris Kelly – thank you for showing me what it means to share and give space to others; to

Paul McLean for your hospitality, for making San Francisco my second home and for always including me; to Ernest Holm Svendsen for listening to me without judgment – thank you for your patience with me and honesty; to Des Brennan for making this book readable in English and for poking fun at me; to Peter Scragg for proof-reading this book with your sharp linguistic eyes; to Greg Scott for encouragement and support to share my experiences in this book; to Tyge Hansen for support and hospitality; to all my dear friends in Denmark who never forgot me while I was away; to my friends in the United States who have supported me and invited me to stay with them during later travels – a long list of people which includes Erin & Chris Ratay, Christine Hansen & Hendi Kaf, Mark Maxon, Shirah Kuschner, Kathy Dailey & Kirk Hulstrom, Jeffrey & Fabrizio Tapia, Shannon & Scott Lindsay, Sharon & Stephen Burns and Francine Osikowicz & David Roccaforte; to the BMW dealerships in the United States who took such good care of me whenever I stopped by; and to all the wonderful people I met along the way who supported me and helped me open my eyes and see the world in a different way. Without you, none of this would have happened.

Contents

Acknowledgments iii

Foreword vii

Introduction xi

THE END — Authenticity and Truth 1

An open heart
Trust 6

Choice of motorcycle
Express who you are 25

Luggage
Travel light 36

ON THE ROAD — Vulnerability and Strength 57

Route planning
Stick to your own business 62

Riding techniques
Engage fully 82

Keeping warm
Relax 105

Problem solving
Accept 117

    Maintenance and system relief
    Be still 129

THE BEGINNING — Innocence & Openness 141

    Accidents and first aid
    Yield 144

    Crossing the finish line
    Share 161

Afterword **179**

Foreword

On a crisp, late afternoon in spring, my dog and I had settled into a quiet camping spot along a small mountainside in rural Mississippi in the southeastern part of the United States, when with a quiet rush a motorcyclist pulled in nearby. The lone rider quickly unpacked gear and set up a small tent. Being a social Southerner, I decided to offer my new neighbor a cold beer from an ice box in the back of my truck, and share some firewood.

To my pleasant surprise, the grateful traveler turned out to be one of the most easy-going yet quietly intense women with whom I have crossed paths in my travels around the country and world. It was a synchronicity of fellow travelers sharing food, drink, and company while swapping amazing experiences from faraway lands beside a crackling open fire.

Yet her tale, only part of which is shared in this journal, gave me pause. I know that in between the insights and openness, which don't always come easily, were untold thoughts which she pondered, and feelings that were kept close to her amazed heart.

I wasn't surprised at any of this, not even her passion for her often-uncomfortable mode of travel, at least not at first. But it was obviously both challenging and exhilarating, this self-induced exile from her Other World. It was so much more than a mere adventure.

Within thirty six hours, after much laughter and having delved quickly and deeply into local "soul" food, a bouncing pick-up truck drive along the shores of the mighty Mississippi River, and late-night sharing of the haunting Blues music of the Mississippi Delta, Annette would be off again, continuing her solo journey of proving herself to herself.

This small book is a sometimes-shy, often-defiant celebration of a lone human throwing physical comfort to the wind and taking to the Road, across many cultures in search of something elusive, and in the process becoming part of the road itself. Every unique individual Annette met, every simple meal she shared, every difficulty and every surprising discovery that came her way, has been a tipping point of sorts.

What little bits Annette is sharing in this journal have been cobbled into an age-old tale of a big heart and inquiring mind in search of... well, read on and ponder for yourself.

Felder Rushing
Author of Slow Gardening

Day 24 – January 7, 2007. Rio Gallegos, Argentina

The 150 miles from Piedra Buena to Rio Gallegos were nasty. At this point the landscape was familiar to me: barren Patagonian desert – the Land of Nothingness. The sun was still in bed. It was freezing cold. A brutal side wind numbed my right leg and tore my shoulders and neck apart. Only with great effort did I hold onto my bike.

Then something strange happened. Suddenly I didn't feel Mother Nature's harsh caresses. The wind and cold penetrated my body and yet it didn't affect me. It was as if I accessed a different dimension where I was able to continue riding into eternity. In this dimension there is no goal to be reached, no final destination. I'm already where I need to be. Past, present and future merge. Anything is possible. No, I can't describe it. It has to be experienced.

It's like finding the centre of a circle. No matter how big or small a circle it's got a centre. The centre is exactly where it needs to be. It doesn't need to be moved to the right, up or down. It is the centre. It just is. Nothing more.

Today I experienced this "isness". I am. I am complete. Outside this dimension the wind and cold still penetrate my body but it doesn't affect me. I'm exactly where I need to be.

x

INTRODUCTION

Knowing yourself is to be rooted in Being, instead of lost in your mind.

Eckhart Tolle

On many occasions in my life I've arrived at a point where I've thought: is this it? Whenever I reached a goal, it was with the unspoken expectation that when *this* has been achieved *then* my life will be great. It didn't happen. I never felt fulfilled, at least not for very long. My problems caught up with me, seemingly using GPS and traveling with the speed of light.

I tried to stay clear but when I got divorced at the age of thirty I had had enough. I needed to change direction but I had no idea how or where to begin.

Without any plan or gain in mind I decided to make a childhood dream of riding a motorcycle come true and this decision had a bigger impact on my life than I could imagine. Eight months after I passed the motorcycle test I quit my job as a lawyer in Denmark, sold my belongings, moved to Buenos Aires in Argentina and took unpaid employment in a motorcycle repair shop to learn motorcycle mechanics. When I arrived in Buenos Aires I didn't speak Spanish or know anything about motorcycle mechanics. I had never owned a motorcycle.

In Buenos Aires I bought my first motorcycle, a six-year-old white and black BMW F 650 GS Dakar. After eight months in the repair shop I began a one-year solo motorcycle journey through Latin America.

I was living my dream. I didn't have to worry about money or obligations. Before leaving Denmark I had sold most of my belongings: the house was sold during my divorce and later I sold my car and halved my furniture, jewelry and other inventory of value. I had cut myself loose and for the first time in my life I allowed myself to do what *I* wanted to do. Yet I continued to be caught by the same problems I had tried to leave behind. Slowly, I realized that it wasn't so much *what* I did that was of importance, but *how* I did it.

Whenever I did something, not as a means to an end, but out of delight of doing that particular thing, I experienced a joy and effortlessness that to begin with felt foreign to me. When I gave up controlling events, things came to me instead of me working hard to get them. And when I put everything on the line, when I gave myself completely without holding back, I was rewarded. In those moments, I accessed a gentle and invisible power where I felt blissful and safe even though I was maneuvering through unknown territory.

Until I started riding a motorcycle I was unaware of these moments and what they offered. I had had glimpses of them, but I never let them sink in. I was always on my way, getting somewhere, not paying attention to what I was doing.

Once I left Buenos Aires on my motorcycle I spent hours on roads that didn't know what "bend" or "twist" was. All I had to do was keep my right hand in a light grip around the throttle, pull it back till I reached the speed I wanted and keep it there.

During the first 2,000 miles from Buenos Aires to the southern tip of South America the landscape changed from flat Argentinean Pampas (the word "pampa" comes from the Indian language, Quechua, meaning "plain") to flat Patagonian desert. I'm not sure how the word "Patagonia" helps describe the topography of the landscape. However, if I acknowledge the commonly accepted root of the word "patagon" – from Spanish meaning a "large, clumsy foot", it describes how I felt at the beginning of my journey. Once in a while I passed another vehicle, which put a smile on my face in the desert, but before I knew it, I was alone again. Even though I was moving, I was literally stuck – with myself.

For the most part, being stuck with myself was an unhappy experience. It was disconcerting because with nowhere to run I became aware of how uninspiring my thoughts were. At first I was amazed about how hopelessly dull and repetitive they were but as time passed I got more impressed with their persistence and ability to create emotional turmoil within me. They came out of nowhere, never tiring or slowing down.

I couldn't stop them no matter how hard I tried. In the beginning of my journey it was only after ten hours on the bike that they left me alone. When I reached a point beyond exhaustion they gave me a rest. Those few moments, when I had burned myself down and my mind went quiet, were worth all the agonizing hours on the bike in my own company.

As I made my way through the South American continent I began to experience these moments without reaching a point where I was more dead than alive. I also came to understand that these moments had nothing to do with riding a motorcycle. Riding a motorcycle just happened to be my first consistent entry point to this dimension of being.

This book is about those moments, those moments when we move effortlessly through life and how they come about. Effortless living is not something that can be achieved through determination and hard work. It is something that is allowed to happen.

Chronologically the book doesn't follow the time line of the outer motorcycle journey. Each chapter describes a quality of effortlessness I discovered during my change of career path and solo motorcycle journey. Ironically, these discoveries and realizations came through experiences that were anything but effortless. Every one of them came to me after intense emotional suffering at different times during the journey.

I often chose the road of most resistance but I don't regret a thing. I couldn't have done it differently. It was my path. However, now I take the road of least resistance.

I realize that choosing the road of least resistance – to live effortlessly – may sound like a shock-horror scenario to many: that we should give up and not bother. But living effortlessly doesn't mean that I stop applying myself, stop participating or avoid challenges and difficult situations. On the contrary, it's about applying myself and participating in a way that is right for me. Each one of us has our own way of doing things and our own path to follow. When we trust our natural responses, we live effortlessly.

THE END

AUTHENTICITY AND TRUTH

Day 1 – December 15, 2006. Pinamar, Argentina

In Pinamar I found a campground. It didn't look inviting but I was tired and fed up with riding around trying to find a more appealing place to camp. A campsite cost two bucks and I could pick any of the unoccupied sites. I chose one next to a site with a giant RV, which according to the camping office was owned by an Italian.

Not more than two minutes passed before a man stuck his head out of a window in the RV and asked if I needed help putting up my tent. I happily accepted his offer. I feared the tent business could be a challenge. However, together we smoothly put up the tent and I was relieved that a Ph.D. in outdoor life wasn't required for this task. Here, lawyers stood a chance too.

The Italian offered me a place to sleep in his RV, which I kindly refused. To tell the truth, I was more than satisfied with my new little house. Only once before had I slept in a tent. It was on the island of Anholdt in Denmark with a girlfriend of mine. It was a great holiday despite the rain but I don't remember the tent experience being a success. As far as I recall the tent was leaky.

It didn't look like it was going to rain this evening and I looked forward to my first night in my tent. After we put up the tent Carlo, the Italian, invited me for a cup of tea in his RV where he lived with his Rottweiler, Romelo.

Carlo turned out to be quite a character. He spoke non-stop for three hours and it wasn't only trivial stuff I learned from him. To begin with, Carlo had a gun and a shotgun. The gun was for personal protection and the shotgun (which was of the kind you need a serious weapon permit to possess in Europe) was for shooting empty beer bottles. I didn't comment on the latter piece of information.

The RV weighed almost four and a half tons, had six wheels, six beds (of which Carlo and Romelo each occupied one, the remaining four being filled with garbage), kitchen with a gas cooker, a toilet, a shower and a hundred gallon water tank. The year was vintage – 1978 – and the whole lot cost 8,000 bucks.

Carlo went on to tell me that he was thirty-six years old, had been married twice (I can't beat that – yet), first to a Swedish woman (his Swedish was excellent) and then to an Argentinean. After the separation from his Argentinean wife he left Buenos Aires because an exaggerated cocaine abuse threatened to flush him down the toilet.

Apparently, the cocaine in this part of the world is high quality stuff. Cocaine is delivered in small bags each containing one and a half grams, which is enough for fifteen lines. Most people take two lines to get high but Carlo sniffed all fifteen straight up his nose before noon (according to Carlo this is not good news for your nose). In the afternoon he opened a second bag, which he emptied before his soon to be ex-wife came home from work. Carlo consumed the content of the bags with a side order of whisky, vodka or other hard liquor while he feverishly zapped from one TV-channel to the next. He kept this routine going for six months until his heart started racing. Then he decided to quit. He bought the dog and the RV, sublet his apartment, changed his telephone number and did cold turkey. Just like that.

After this monologue my head was giddy. At nine o'clock I withdrew to my new house and fell asleep at once. I slept surprisingly well considering it had been ten years since I last slept in a tent. My inflatable mini-mattress was great. However, during the night it got a bit damp in the tent but presumably it didn't help that I slept with my sleeping bag inside out. Clever.

An open heart
Trust

Trust the instinct to the end,
though you can render no reason.

Ralph Waldo Emerson

For a long time I believed that the best way to go nowhere was to procrastinate. To some extent I still believe it's true but I've realized that there is a more efficient way to get stuck that is often the cause of procrastination: to lack trust in oneself.

Trust is the basic ingredient of effortlessness like flour is in baking a good loaf of bread. Without it I'm unable to absorb and respond to the changing and unreliable circumstances surrounding me. Trust allows me to open up and experience every moment anew and the abundance that truly exists everywhere.

The trust I'm speaking of is not trust in myself as my personality or my thoughts and emotions. They are forever changing and unreliable. It's a trust that runs deeper; it runs to the core of my being. This trust allows me to take action in ways that are not otherwise possible. It's a trust that allows actions to be conducted based on incomplete information about the case in hand. It cuts through the chatterbox in my head as well as my feelings and emotions and enables me to listen to the voice deep within.

For many years I lacked trust in myself. I felt that everyone else knew better, also when it concerned my own matters: what to do with my life, what opinions to have, what to express and what not to express. I believed I had no authority in my life and to get what I wanted I had to compromise myself and use manipulation and control.

Growing up I felt vulnerable and insecure and I had a great need to protect this inner fragility. At any cost I wanted to avoid allowing others to see me as I was and to avoid expressing what was going on inside me. I felt that if I let my guard down I would be ridiculed and rejected.

The feeling of vulnerability created a great deal of inner emotional turmoil. In response I built a thick wall around me that would have made any medieval king envious. I allowed no-one to get close to me. An attempt to get in would be met with either attack or immediate reinforcement of the wall.

Inside the wall I tried to escape the turmoil, which ranged in intensity from a sensation of restlessness and discomfort to an abyss threatening to erase my existence. For years I silenced these sensations through excessive eating or through smoking, drinking, watching TV, talking on the phone, shopping for stuff I didn't need – you name it, any activity that could prevent me from facing the blackness inside me.

With this much activity aimed at diverting away from experiencing what went on inside me, it was no wonder I lacked trust in myself and that my sense of direction was shabby. However, at the age of thirty, I consciously listened to the inner voice that had been hidden underneath the turmoil. For the first time in my life I listened openly, without any agenda. Whatever needed to be known I was willing to hear. Once I tuned in I heard the voice loud and clear. The first time it happened it presented me with a simple question in the form of a three-letter word: why?

When the question surfaced I was in Salar de Uyuni, the world's largest salt flat in southern Bolivia. I looked around me. The light was so strong I had to squint my eyes behind my sunglasses. The reflection of the sunbeams in the ten billion tons of salt that surrounded me made me dizzy.

I was in between two law jobs and backpacking through South America for two months. By chance I had ended up on a bus to San Pedro de Atacama in Chile and got talking to a couple of travelers with whom I booked a three-day jeep tour through Salar de Uyuni.

The landscape was so enchanting that I had trouble believing my own eyes. Most of the time I felt I had been beamed into another galaxy. It was mind-bogglingly different from anything I had seen before.

We drove to Isla Incanuasi, a small island in the middle of the salt flat solely inhabited by the cactus family. We were at an altitude of 12,000 feet. I climbed to the far end of the miniature island to escape the talk and noise of the other travelers.

I let the silence and stunning beauty engulf me and looked out on the vast salt plain that covered an area equivalent to a quarter of my native Danish homeland. The blood rushed through my veins as if I had fallen in love. My hands buzzed, my body felt light and my mind was clear. At this point the question surfaced: why? Why had I never done the things *I* had dreamed of? I had achieved the goals I had set for myself but they hadn't been goals or dreams that allowed the expression of my innermost being. They were goals I had set with the aim of fitting in, not giving it any thought whether I was being true to myself or not.

Since I was a little girl, as far back as I can remember, I had dreamt of riding a motorcycle. Growing up I didn't know anyone who rode one. Every year I watched a parade of motorcycles pass my childhood home to mark the opening in spring and closing in fall of the world's oldest existing amusement park north of Copenhagen. For a couple of hours it was impossible to cross the road. Thousands of motorcycles in all shapes and sizes took over the road and on this occasion the police made sure they had right of way.

Two police motorcycles formed the head and tail of the big snake of motorcycles, which slowly made its way out of Copenhagen and north along the Øresund Straight that separates Denmark and Sweden. At every intersection along the nine-mile ride, the traffic lights were switched off and the police blocked the side roads. With regular intervals a police motorcycle appeared, being the odd one out in its attempt to keep the snake under control.

Every motorcycle brand, old and new, was represented in the parade but it was the few custom-built bikes that particularly caught my attention. They were loud and shining with all their chrome. Hardly any of the riders wore helmets. During the parade the police let them get away with it. I heard these bikes come from a far distance and I eagerly anticipated them, trying to imagine what they looked like. I was never disappointed.

As the motorcycles roared past me I promised myself that one day – one day when I was old enough – I would be on one of them.

Now I had reached thirty and I wasn't any closer to riding a motorcycle except for being legally old enough to ride one. Instead, I had "celebrated" my thirtieth birthday by having an argument with my husband, with me finishing off the quarrel shouting: "If this ends in divorce, I'll tear you apart" – or something along those lines.

After a couple of months of phony attempts on both sides to fix the damage it did end in divorce. One evening I stood in the bathroom in our house that was too big for two people, looking at myself in the mirror thinking: "Oh shit

– what if we actually manage to solve our problems?" That's when it dawned on me that I should stop trying.

Six weeks after my husband and I had signed the separation papers, something happened that led me to Salar de Uyuni.

I was in Berlin for a law conference. I had invited one of my brothers to join me and we arrived the day before the conference started and had a stroll around Mitte. The night before we had both been up late and the seven-hour car journey from Copenhagen had drained us of our last energy. We decided to have dinner at the hotel. The food was tasty, though a bit on the heavy side, unsurprisingly for the German cuisine. The conversation was pleasant. Well, at least until my brother more or less at random changed the topic of conversation.

"So, do you think you might meet any interesting people at the conference tomorrow?"

"If you mean "men" then the answer is no."

"You never know what might happen."

"Maybe not, but I'm absolutely sure that *that* won't happen. I'm not interested in having some random fling."

"But maybe it would be good for you to get out there again."

"Look," I said defensively, "I know *exactly* what's best for me and that's the end of that."

The next morning I arrived at the conference and as I entered the small conference room, my eyes caught sight of a breathtakingly handsome man. Shaken, I passed him and found a seat a couple of rows in front of him. I fought the urge to turn around and look at him until my memory brought up the image of a big house in Copenhagen containing one human being soon to be known as my ex-husband and a pile of unresolved problems. In an instant, that took care of the urge to stare and I decided to avoid any contact with that man.

My plan worked well during the morning lecture. At the first break I went outside the conference room, poured myself a cup of coffee and stood around. I had no desire to mingle. I felt my life was in ruins. I didn't even know who I was anymore. I could state the obvious – name, sex, occupation but besides that I was blank.

At this exact time my plan received its first blow. The handsome man came up to me and started a conversation. I couldn't believe it. Here I was, determined to mind my own business and then this man had the nerve to approach me and spoil my master plan.

I wish I could tell you about the content of our conversation but I didn't listen to anything he said. I caught the fact that he was half European, half South American as well as a few details about his work. That was it. I experienced a pull towards him so strong that all I did was stare at him, trying to grasp the radiance of his presence. It wasn't possible so my system shut down my sense of hearing and any related brain activity it might have caused. I suspect it also had an impact on the few sounds that escaped the hole in my face situated below my nose and that they didn't reveal any form of intelligence on my part.

At lunchtime I met up with my brother and escaped any form of interaction with the rest of the group – including *that* man. Both relieved and excited I left the building and walked around the corner to the café on Gendarmenmarkt where my brother waited.

"So, did you meet any interesting people?" my brother asked with a cheeky smile.

I sat down and as casually as possible gave him the light version.

"Well, there was a guy who looked quite nice but nothing special," I heard myself saying and changed the subject. I still had a chance to save the remains of my master plan and any dignity I might have left after the conversation with my brother the night before.

However, when I got back to the conference and this man eagerly asked me where I'd been for lunch I knew all hope was lost. I was going down the toilet along with my master plan whether I liked it or not.

We spent the weekend together in Berlin and I was on cloud nine though my hearing never recuperated from the first blow. Our conversations are lost to me. I only remember him saying that he was planning a trip to South America the following year. I also remember when we said goodbye.

We were standing in front of Potzdamer Platz subway entrance under a clear blue sky. He was on his way to a soccer game. I asked him if we could meet up before I headed back to

Copenhagen. He hesitantly answered that it didn't fit into his plans.

Before he could add anything the words "your loss" came out of my mouth. I gave him a kiss, turned around and walked away. Just like that. I kept walking without looking back, taking one step after another while feeling my life tumbling down on me. Each step away from him was a step into darkness. By the time I reached my hotel even the clear sky above me was hidden by clouds.

I arrived back in Copenhagen a different person. The ending of my marriage had made a big hole in my protective wall and I had come face to face with my vulnerability. While my guard was down this half South American man had slipped in. However, the wounds from my recent separation were so fresh that even the slightest disturbance could make me fall apart. I didn't know how to cope and it left me with one option: denial. I felt too fragile to allow the feeling of rejection to be truly felt so I pretended he hadn't turned me down and focused solely on the bliss I had experienced during our time together.

With this focus I felt alive again after having been numb for months under the weight of marital problems. I felt I had been resurrected. The experience of bliss and joy in Berlin that had been absent in my life for years made me ecstatic and I fled into a dream about a man that only existed in my imagination. At this point I was unable to separate my blissful experiences in Berlin from him and the belief that he had caused it. It desperately made me want to see him again. In hindsight, I realize that I tried to use him as an escape. Luckily he was clever enough to stay clear of me. He wrote to me that he didn't want to be in contact with me and outwardly I respected his wish while a dream about a future "us" grew within me.

The attention I gave to the idea of this man quickly gathered momentum. Before I knew it I was trying to create an opportunity to meet him again.

With his brief remark about his plans to go to South America in mind, two and a half months after my trip to Berlin, I bought a plane ticket to South America. The greatest part of my motivation was undoubtedly an eagerness, despite having been turned down, to create an opportunity for encountering him. However, it didn't occur to me to narrow down my operating field to less than the South American continent or indeed contact him to find out if and when he would be in South America.

I needed time out. I needed to remove myself from my situation and get a new perspective, new input to help me move forward in a different direction. I needed to go somewhere I hadn't been before and that need had an irresistible pull on me.

Until meeting the half South American man I had never considered going to South America. That part of the world didn't interest me. It was the last place on earth I wanted to travel to on my own yet there I was, sitting in Salar de

Uyuni in southern Bolivia blown away by the immense beauty of the landscape before me.

As I sat in the salt flat I thought about my childhood dream of riding a motorcycle. I had turned thirty and I hadn't taken the motorcycle test. I had put it off because I was busy getting somewhere in my life, involved in achieving another goal I had set for myself, passing an exam or finding a better job. In that moment I realized that I would never take the test if I didn't act now. So right there, in the salt flat of Uyuni, I promised myself to take the test when I returned to Denmark.

A month later I was back in Copenhagen, had started a new job in a law firm and as chance would have it, on my new route to work, I passed a motorcycle driving school. Every day I rode past it on my bicycle without going in. I intended to check out other schools before signing up but after a week had gone by I hadn't done my research. I was procrastinating and letting my dream fade away again.

I thought about the promise I had made to myself in the salt flat in Bolivia and in a flicker of desperation I thought: to hell with it. This might be the worst and most expensive place in the world to take the motorcycle test but I don't care. I'm going in and I'm signing up.

The driving school turned out to be excellent and inexpensive. Three months later I had taken all the lessons and passed the tests. I felt I could fly. My childhood dream had come true. Now, I needed some wheels.

Shortly after I had dinner with a friend of mine who is also a lawyer. As always the conversation turned into a discussion of what we would like to do instead of working in law. I told him that I didn't have a clue. All I knew was that I wanted to travel in South America, ride a motorcycle and learn Spanish. Upon hearing this, my friend suggested that I do all of those things in one go.

When I heard his suggestion, I instantly knew I had to do it. For the first time in my life I knew without a shred of doubt what I had to do even though it hardly made sense. I mean, I had to quit my job, leave my legal career and sell my belongings – for what? A crazy idea that felt right. Yep. I had no fear about making the necessary changes because I knew it was right.

A brief encounter with a half South American and a conversation with a good friend had set something in motion that was much bigger than myself. After that, everything fell into place.

The following week I bought a plane ticket to Buenos Aires, Argentina. I had two weeks vacation coming up and I wanted to rent a motorcycle in Argentina and find out how it felt traveling alone by motorcycle in South America.

I boarded the plane in Copenhagen with my new driver's license, a borrowed motorcycle jacket and the address of a motorcycle rental shop in Buenos Aires.

The day after my arrival in Buenos Aires I took a taxi from my hostel to the motorcycle shop. I would be lying if I said I wasn't nervous.

For all I knew, the people in the motorcycle shop could be gangsters or mass murderers. In Denmark, some motorcycle riders were sketchy but this was Buenos Aires, the real South America. I couldn't even begin to imagine what kind of riders they had down here.

My train of thought was interrupted. The taxi stopped and on the other side of the street I saw the shop. "Motocare" it said in big yellow letters on an orange background. A row of motorcycles was parked outside the shop. I paid the taxi driver and took a moment to inspect the shop from a distance. No dead bodies lying around. Good start.

I crossed the heavily trafficked Avenida del Libertador and walked into the shop. Motorcycles in every size and shape filled the room. A bald guy, looking like a gangster, sat behind an untidy desk while talking to a customer. They caught sight of me and fell silent. I later learned that they didn't have many blonde, female customers from Scandinavia.

The bald guy greeted me in Spanish, which threw me a bit. I gathered up courage and stuttered my only but thoroughly rehearsed sentence in Spanish: "Quisiera alquilar una moto." I would like to rent a motorcycle. The bald guy gave an elaborate answer in Spanish and I tried to explain in English that I didn't understand a word.

So it went back and forth until he made a phone call and passed the phone on to me. I stared at the phone as if it was the first time I had seen a cordless telephone. Then in English he said: "Speak." I put the phone to my ear and let out a careful "hello?" To my pleasant surprise I heard the voice of a man speaking fluent English. It was the owner of Motocare, Mariano. He asked me if I could wait ten minutes, then he would be at the shop. Considering the fact that it had taken me twenty hours to get there, I didn't see why not.

We talked over the rental and I decided to rent a Honda Transalp 600 for ten days. He lent me a helmet, a pair of riding pants and gloves. Two days later I picked up the bike, twisted the throttle and rode west. I was scared beyond the edge of reason but I knew I was at a point of no return.

The motorcycle journey blew my mind. I loved it. I felt alive and free. I was happy without giving it any thought. I felt I had been beamed out of ordinary life into a road movie where every experience was loaded with juice and vitality. I spent all ten days alone with my rented motorcycle and Robert Pirsig's "Zen and the Art of Motorcycle Maintenance", hardly speaking to anyone, just riding through the beautiful Argentinean landscape.

The journey was a huge success but it took its toll. I went beyond my limitations and it left me exhausted. When I returned to Denmark I was bedridden for two weeks with a high fever. I slept most of the time while digesting my Argentinean motorcycle adventure.

I was changing and whatever went on inside me disturbed me quite a bit. In fact, it disturbed me to such an extent that I called a therapist I had seen during my divorce, explained my situation and asked if she thought I was going insane. I heard dry but reassuring and friendly laughter. She told me that the anxiety I experienced was normal and to be expected in a situation like mine where I was pulling the rug away from under my own feet.

The prospect of not going insane helped cheer me up. I realized that during my ride across Argentina I had experienced a glimpse of what life could be like without the layers I had built up over the course of my first thirty years. I had relied on these layers to keep myself together and safe but during my divorce I got a first hand experience of how fragile they were.

This realization provided me with a strong urge to shed them all and find out what I was hiding underneath. Building layers was my way of protecting myself and fitting in. As far back as I could remember I had tried to fit in and sought the approval of others but despite my efforts I never succeeded. I was sick and tired of hiding and pretending to be something I wasn't. I wanted to do something that felt right to *me* – not because it was the sensible thing to do or it looked good on my résumé.

I was back in my office in the law firm. I looked at the case files on my desk and felt worn out. I thought about my plan to go back to South America. To pull it off I knew I had to learn something about motorcycle mechanics and learning Spanish wouldn't be a disadvantage either. Instead of reaching for a file I opened my mailbox and wrote an e-mail to the owner of the motorcycle shop in Buenos Aires. I asked him if he knew a place in Buenos Aires where I could learn how to repair motorcycles.

The next day I got a reply. He wrote: "The question is easy to answer, you can learn many and the most common repairs in our shop if this is fine for you and if you can handle it."

"If you can handle it?" What on earth was that supposed to mean? *Of course* I can handle it!

Four months later I stood in front of my new work place Motocare – a motorcycle shop in Buenos Aires. If someone a year earlier had told me that I would be standing there, I would have thought that the person was insane. But once I was there it felt like the most natural thing in the world. As if it had always been a part of the plan.

More than twenty-five years passed until my dream came true of being one of the riders in the nine-mile ride in the city I was born in. But before it happened, I rode alone through the Americas. When people have asked me how that came about my answer has been: I allowed myself to listen to my heart and took the first step *without the expectation of a future gain*.

Day 178 – June 9, 2007. Salta, Argentina

In Cachi I met a Dutch guy, Wim, in a jeep. Together we drove to San Antonio de los Cobres. The road through the Andes was one of the most spectacular rides I've experienced on my trip. It was wonderful to ride with Wim. I relaxed and enjoyed the ride, knowing that if I needed help it was there. As it happened, I did end up needing his help.

At 15,000 feet I went down in a sharp, sandy curve. I fell on my right where my remaining side case after a crash in Tierra del Fuego was attached. The damage was minimal and Wim helped me pick up Dakar. To ease the ride I took off the side case and my backpack and put them in his jeep. Dakar had lost most of his power in the altitude and so had I. We had crossed a river several times. The first time it was about three feet deep. It was a bit scary but I was glad I could cope.

By the time we got to the pass at 16,000 feet I was altitude sick. It was no fun. I hardly took any photos. I just wanted to get down that damn mountain as quickly as possible. I didn't enjoy the ride down. Bummer.

After seven hours riding, during which time we saw one car, we arrived in San Antonio de los Cobres at 12,400 feet. At this point my head felt as if it was about to explode.

It took us a while to find a hotel with two vacant rooms. The one we found had a big and a small room. Without giving it any thought, I presumed the big room was for me but Wim disagreed. He suggested that we draw lots for the rooms. I thought it was a silly idea but I accepted and lost, just as I expected. I was puzzled about his suggestion but I understood his reason for wanting the big room. After all, he traveled with a small dog.

My altitude sickness got worse and I threw up (this could also have been caused by the rotten tasting water I drank in Cachi – it had a suspicious taste but still I poured it down my drain. Not good). I told Wim that he had to go to the grocery store alone to buy food for dinner. Wim wasn't pleased to hear this. I found his behavior odd but I thought to myself, okay – I shouldn't exaggerate my altitude sickness. I did feel a lot better after I threw up so I guess I could go to the grocery store. Let me here add that Wim wasn't altitude sick.

Luckily, the grocery store was just around the corner and it wasn't an exhausting excursion. I hoped that Wim would offer to cook the meal, but no. Wim didn't want to cook on his own. Instead I did all the chopping and also ended up with the dishes to wash after dinner. Again, I thought that perhaps I demanded too much, expecting him do more of the work because I felt sick.

In the morning we ate breakfast together. I had fetched fresh bread from the grocery store and set the table. Wim squeezed a bunch of oranges and I presumed that some of the juice was for me. But no. Every drop of juice went into Wim's belly. This time I couldn't keep my mouth shut. I found his behavior too selfish, which I indirectly let him know. He seemed to feel caught in the act and began to squeeze the last orange.

At this point I was in a grump and told him that now I didn't want the juice. He stopped the squeezing and that made me think he didn't want it. I poured the juice of the last orange into a cup and expected to drink it but Wim was again one step ahead of me. He grabbed the cup and took a slurp.

I couldn't believe my own eyes. I probably looked surprised, which Wim noticed. I confessed and told him that I was offended that he didn't offer me any juice to begin with and that I got into a grump.

"But that's very silly," he said.

"Just as silly as when you were being selfish," I replied.

The atmosphere turned chilly and I drank the remaining orange juice.

Choice of motorcycle
Express who you are

Greatness is not to be this or that, but to be yourself; and this anyone can do when he wants to.

Søren Kierkegaard

Before I left Denmark I knew what kind of motorcycle I wanted: a BMW F 650 GS Dakar. Why? Because I thought it was beautiful.

A year had passed since my encounter with the half South American man in Berlin. Since my return from my first trip to South America we had been in contact. I still hoped he would change his mind about me and I eagerly fed my dream about a future "us". He was now with another woman so I was aware of the fact that "us" wasn't going to happen any time soon.

I called him to tell him about my South American motorcycle plans. When he heard that I wanted to ride a motorcycle through South America he said: "The bike you need is the BMW F 650 GS Dakar." I had never heard about this motorcycle, in fact I couldn't come up with the name of any motorcycle model.

As I hung up, one of my brothers came by. I told him about my plans too and for the second time within ten minutes I heard the words: "The bike you need is the BMW F 650 GS Dakar."

Strange, I thought. I'd better check out this bike. I went online and googled it. When I saw it, it was love at first sight. I felt I had found my bike.

I looked further into the matter and my initial hunch seemed right. The BMW F 650 GS Dakar would be ideal for the South American terrain. However, the seat was high which is a disadvantage for an inexperienced rider because of the high point of gravity. I decided it would be more sensible to go with the standard version of the BMW F 650 GS. It's identical to the Dakar except for a lower seat level and a smaller front wheel.

When I got to Buenos Aires I asked Mariano, the owner of Motocare, to keep an eye out for a used BMW F 650 GS – the standard version. I hadn't tried it, yet I was determined to get this bike. My colleagues in the motorcycle shop supported my decision.

It turned out to be difficult to find this motorcycle on the second hand market in Buenos Aires and as time passed I considered other bikes. However, my thoughts always returned to the BMW.

After my first month in Buenos Aires without a motorcycle I was desperate for some wheels. I signed up for a one-day motorcycle rider's training course at BMW.

Arriving at the training site I had the choice of riding the standard 650 GS and the Dakar. I told the instructor that I was an inexperienced rider and that it was probably best that I rode the standard 650 GS with the lower seat instead of the Dakar. The instructor agreed and said it would be the right bike for me.

As I got on the bike I was immediately disappointed. I could hardly believe my own experience. The seating position was awkward. It was slow and heavy to handle and it was as much fun to ride as a bathtub on wheels. It didn't feel right at all.

I was shocked. This was supposed to be the right bike for me and I didn't like it. What the hell was going on? My own real time experience had the nerve to go against my idea of the perfect bike for me. What was I supposed to do now? Would I be able to find the right bike when the bike I was convinced would be perfect for me turned out to a disappointment? Did this mean I couldn't trust myself?

There was only one thing to do and the sooner I did it, the better. It was what I always did in situations like this: to rationalize and mould my real time experience in a way that would fit the idea in my head. It never occurred to me that it would be easier to change my mind instead of trying to change reality, which at the end of the day meant trying to change the universe. If I had bothered to check the score of the match "Universe versus Annette Birkmann" the Universe's lead of infinity against zero might have made me consider changing tactics.

I didn't look at the score and I doubt at this point in my life it would have made a difference. I hadn't reached my pain threshold so all I could do was switch on the autopilot. Here's the list of what I believed to be useful and uplifting thoughts designed to match my real time experience with the idea in my head:

- My lack of riding experience has left me disappointed.
- I had too high expectations.
- I don't know anything about bikes.
- Other bikes are probably worse.
- I'm not paying attention.
- I don't know what I'm doing.
- Experienced riders tell me that this is the bike for me. They know better than me.
- I shouldn't be so demanding.
- I've set myself up for failure.
- There's something wrong with me and I need to get on with the program.

For the entire day on the riding course these thoughts went through my head and by the end of the day they had persuaded me that my real time experience was wrong. The BMW F 650 GS was the right bike for me whether I liked it or not. I was going to stick with my choice. End of story.

We had ten minutes left on the course. All day I had felt a strong itch to ride the Dakar but I had been afraid to ask. Maybe the instructor would think it was out of my league, that I wouldn't be able to handle it and that I might injure myself and damage the bike. In the end I couldn't help myself. I *had* to try it to put my mind to rest, to know that the Dakar was impossible for me to handle.

I got on the Dakar, kicked the side stand up, pressed the ignition and put it in gear. As I let go of the clutch and twisted the throttle, I *knew* I had found my bike. A surge of joy went through my body. It blew my mind. The two bikes are almost identical. The engines *are* identical, everything on the two bikes is alike except for the seat level and the size of the front wheel. But for me it made a world of a difference. The Dakar was fun to ride. I enjoyed myself, I felt at ease and safe. I wasn't in doubt. The instructor also noticed the difference in my riding. "That's your bike," he said "I can tell you're having much more fun riding it than the other one."

When I tried the Dakar all confusion dropped away. My mind wasn't busy making lists of pros and cons. It felt right and the doubtful voices in my head disappeared.

It was like experiencing water for the first time. The word "water" says nothing about what water is. Any description, however precise, can't bring me to know what water is. Only by experiencing water myself do I realize what it is. I don't need any words or thoughts for knowing. It's the same when I taste something for the first time. I don't have to think about whether I like it or not. The answer comes instantaneously. It doesn't mean that the answer is an expression of what is permanently true for me. The only permanency in life is change but when I'm open to every moment I allow myself the full experience of it.

It seems to me that when in doubt, I need to go beyond thinking. My thoughts cannot tell me what's right for me. They can only give me an explanation or interpretation of how I feel. More thinking won't help. This leaves two options: be still or take action. If being still doesn't give me an answer, I take action. If taking action doesn't give me an answer, I become still. When I step out of my stream of thoughts, whatever step I take either leads me one step closer to clarity or I get pushed back and learn something to help me move forward.

In South America, I've met people on heavy cruisers and fast sports bikes, neither seemingly being the perfect choice for exploring a continent where dirt roads are more common than paved roads. I've also met people on bikes of small and unknown motorcycle brands. It's my guess that you're more likely to find spare parts for these types of bikes in a different solar system than in South America. Once I met a guy whose traveling buddy carried a full size surfboard on his bike on a ride from San Francisco to the southern tip of South America. He wanted to combine his passion for riding a motorcycle with his passion for surfing. I've no idea how he coped on his bike in side wind. I guess he went surfing.

But that's the thing. It's not about choosing the ideal bike or mode of travel but allowing the free expression of one's being. Of course there are advantages when I choose a bike that can handle the roads I'm planning to take. The ride on a bumpy dirt road will feel smoother on a bike with a flexible suspension than on a bike with a stiff suspension. I also reduce the risk of crashing when my bike is designed to handle the roads I'm taking. However, I don't believe the advantages can outweigh the depressing inner resistance I'll experience if I ride a bike that doesn't fit me.

I've spent many hours on my motorcycle. During my journey it became my best friend. If I don't enjoy the time I spend on my bike what's the point of doing the trip? So I can say to my friends that I've *done* Bolivia and Brazil by motorcycle? It might give me instant gratification but it won't be long before the feeling dampens.

When I choose the bike that fits me I might not be able to go down every road I encounter. However, on the roads I *can* take I'll enjoy the riding experience to the fullest. What seems like a limitation at first turns out to be the doorway to fully expressing who I am. Isn't that the point of the journey anyway?

Other people can guide me and have opinions about my choice of motorcycle but at the end of the day they can't *know* what's right for me. As Shirley Bassey sings in the Propellerhead's "History repeating":

"Some people don't dance, if they don't know who's singing; why ask your head, it's your hips that are swinging."

For me, finding the "right" motorcycle is not a willful act of choosing one thing over another but the spontaneous relaxation into "what is". And with the "right" bike, the rest is detail. Whatever continent I want to explore is open to me and I will be able to find *my* way to get through.

Day 87 – March 11, 2007. Villa de Angostura, Argentina

I'm so tired. I've hardly slept for three weeks. Perhaps I should stop traveling, throw in the towel, go home, be unemployed, find a job in law and complain about it till the end of my life: a life that I will live in loneliness because I've become bitter and have pushed everyone around me away. Ugh. I'm on the verge of crying. I'm sitting in a crappy restaurant, where I've eaten a piece of gross apple pie and drunk a dull cup of coffee. I better leave before my mind is completely consumed by darkness. I wish I didn't have to return to the dorm at the hostel. I wish I had my own room where I would be able to be alone.

I chose this restaurant because it's got Internet but my laptop can't find the websites I'm trying to access. The connection seems to be working but I'm not online. It's probably best that way. I don't want to hear from anyone or anything. I just want to be left alone.

I don't want to continue living life on a rollercoaster. I'm so tired of it. In fact I'm able to throw up over myself in thigh-wide beams. It's just wonderful to feel this way. It's just great. I'm living my dream and I just want to throw up because I'm so fed up with my life. Perhaps I'm already tired of traveling. I couldn't care less about all the things I see. It's as if my motorcycle journey has become a pretext. A scene I arrange for the world while I, behind the curtain, do nothing. A bit like the knitting I've now bought. I don't want to do anything at all. I just want to be alone and empty in my head. Everyone is running around having to see this and that – always trying to hunt down a new experience, another way of building a self-image. Is that a lot better than being at home and going to work every day? I doubt it. People are constantly seeking something they never seem to find. I'm no better myself. My travel blog is a mere show of how I would like to be perceived. I don't feel like updating it anymore. I don't want to write about how fabulous I feel when in reality I'm not feeling fabulous at all, when I don't give a damn about any of my experiences.

I often feel I'm on the right track, but am I? Perhaps I'm heading straight for a big black hole I'll never be able to get out of? Perhaps I'll end up going insane? Maybe that's not such a bad thing. At least I'll be unaware of the trouble of living. Then I'll be able to be a nut in my own nutty world where I'm the only one who understands what's going on. But isn't that what's happening already – to all of us? We don't even understand what's going on in our own tiny world. We're lonely and scared and we try to hide behind a multitude of masks. What would happen if we threw away our masks? If we lived freely? It would be wonderful. And it's so simple, yet it seems so difficult.

Yesterday, I went to the hairdresser. I asked to have my hair cut and have my highlights replaced with a dark dough-colored shade. It was not a charming color but I believe it's the one that matches my real hair color the most. The male hairdresser was in shock and couldn't believe that I wanted to leave the blonde look behind. Admittedly, I have to get used to the new color. It ain't pretty but I suppose it's some kind of outer expression of my attempt to find myself – the natural me: to be who I am, as I am.

Luggage
Travel light

*The real voyage of discovery consists
not in seeking new landscapes
but in having new eyes.*

Marcel Proust

If someone were to ask me today what to pack for a long distance motorcycle journey my answer would be: as little as possible.

It's been my experience that the less weight I have on the bike the easier it is to handle. If the bike is easy to handle I reduce the risk of having an accident. It's that simple.

If I realize down the road that I need something I haven't packed, then as long as I'm traveling on Planet Earth I will be able to get hold of something that will meet my needs. I might have to go out of my way to get it and it might not be exactly what I had envisioned, but if I need it, I'll find it. If I can't find it, I don't need it. This means I might have to change my plans. If I'm unwilling to do that, I'm stuck. However, I'm not stuck because I can't find what I need but because I don't want to change my mind about where I think I need to go.

This leads me to a crucial distinction in the luggage department. I believe there are two types of luggage: physical luggage and mental luggage. Too much physical luggage is a pain in the neck but it's usually not enough to immobilize myself. For this, I need the mental luggage, so let's start here.

The mental luggage

A journalist once asked me if there was anytime during my journey where I thought: "I have never imagined *this* happening." The immediate answer that came to mind was: "All the time!" But once I said it I realized that it wasn't true. No matter where I went, in every experience there was something familiar to me: myself.

Even if I had tried I wouldn't have been able to get further away from my usual surroundings in Denmark. The difference between working in a conservative law firm in Copenhagen and a motorcycle repair shop in Buenos Aires was considerable. Not only did the physical work places bear little resemblance to each other but also my colleagues and the clients and customers seemed to originate from different planets.

I had four colleagues at the motorcycle shop: the owner who spoke fluent English and three other Argentinean men who only spoke Spanish.

When I arrived on my first day at work I realized that I wasn't the only one who had anticipated this day. I hardly recognized the shop from my first visit six months earlier. The desk was tidy, the repair shop was spotless clean and every tool was in its place. The owner had even asked the mechanic to mix cement and fix a hole in the floor in the back room.

When the introductions had been made I was left with the Spanish-speaking mechanic, drinking maté – a bitter, caffeine-loaded herbal tea that is very popular in Argentina. The mechanic was working on a big thing I suspected was a part from a motorcycle. He eagerly explained something about it.

After half an hour the owner dropped in on us and realized the hopelessness of the situation. Apparently, the mechanic had been explaining how a carburetor works but since I didn't know what a carburetor was and didn't understand a word of Spanish my learning curve didn't take off. Instead the owner suggested that the mechanic showed me how to take off a wheel.

Through the "monkey-see, monkey-do" technique I got into the rhythms of the motorcycle repair shop away from anything I had done before. I was thrilled and the guys at the shop eagerly taught me the ropes. I would be lying if I claimed it wasn't a challenge. The challenge, however, was of a different nature than expected.

It was demanding to take up a new occupation in a big city I didn't know, in a different part of the world with a different culture, a language I didn't speak and where most people didn't speak the languages I did. I felt different and I looked different too. Being tall and blonde I stuck out everywhere I went. Once I got a motorcycle I believe I was classified as "alien of unknown origin".

However, the real challenge was dealing with the mental luggage I brought with me and avoiding falling back into my old habits. In this respect I wasn't coping very well. Soon after I arrived in Buenos Aires my old ways of thinking and behaving forced me back into a way of living that I knew only too well and that produced the kind of painful experiences I wanted to leave behind.

In Danish we have a saying: "The gnome follows you wherever you go". I experienced the truth of this after a couple of weeks in Buenos Aires. My gnome had made a quick move. I saw it coming, I felt it coming and I desperately wanted to avoid it. Yet I was unable to respond appropriately to the challenge. I didn't understand the nature and cause of the challenge. Consequently, I had to deal with the same issues as usual.

My biggest challenge was facing my eagerness to fit in and seek approval. I wanted to get away from the materialism and focus on status that has a tendency to flourish amongst lawyers. I didn't want to dress up for work and hide underneath expensive labels or spend time on shopping in an attempt to build an image of myself, which had nothing to do with who I was.

My efforts to change direction lasted two weeks. Then I went clothes shopping the first time. I bought a nice skirt and blouse, a handbag and a pair of high-heeled boots. A couple of weeks later I put on mascara and lip gloss for work in the repair shop.

None of these things I did for myself, at least only to a small extent. I had launched myself into a male dominated culture that had an outlook on women I wasn't used to in Scandinavia. I experienced an enormous focus on looks and appearance and men seemed not only to notice every detail about women but also allowed themselves to comment on it.

I bought into the whole package. I liked the attention. At home I was pretty much "Index 100". In Scandinavia you see thousands of women with the same features as me. Now, I was suddenly different and something special and whenever I got a compliment, it fed a need inside me for one more. I wanted to fit in *and* be special and different.

By trying to fit in and seek approval I ignored what was right for me. I stopped being true to myself, which had been the purpose of going away in the first place. Instead of preparing for my big trip ahead and engaging myself in my dream project I was more concerned about pleasing people around me, trying to live up to what I thought was their idea about what kind of person I should be. I used the attention I got to guide me: the more attention I got, the more I thought I fitted in.

I quickly lost interest in learning motorcycle mechanics after the first thrill of doing something different had disappeared. I found it difficult to stay excited about having dirt under my fingernails "in the office". The novelty of dirt has a limited life span – even in Buenos Aires.

In the beginning I loved being away from the computer, not sitting in front of a screen and shuffle papers around. I enjoyed helping out the mechanic, learning about the different spare parts and tools. The mechanic and I communicated with the help of my pocket book dictionary and whenever we met a dead end, we called the owner to help us out and translate.

It was a wonderful and innocent way to immerse myself into a new language. It was playful and fun. With private language lessons in the mornings I quickly made progress. In the afternoon I picked up a rich supplement of words they didn't teach at language school. Here I'm not only talking about words for motorcycle parts and tools but also rude Spanish-Argentinean slang. My vocabulary in this area of the Spanish language flourished. Even my language teachers were impressed.

After a month in the repair shop I started spending less time with the mechanic and more time in front of the computer, emailing friends and surfing the Internet. I did the odd jobs for the owner and ran errands but I hardly worked in the repair shop. I forgot why I had come to the repair shop – to learn about motorcycle mechanics and prepare for my journey.

My efforts to seek approval and fit in consumed most of my energy and yet they produced no effect. I was continuing down the same road I'd followed for years. It was my religion. Try harder. Fit in or die.

Seven and a half months passed before I realized that something was wrong. It hadn't escaped my attention that I had become increasingly unhappy, I just didn't know what to do about it. It never dawned on me that it wasn't important to fit in and win other people's approval. I knew I was responsible for my own happiness, I just didn't know how to take this responsibility upon myself. I believed that I had to take care of everybody else's happiness (by trying to live up to what I thought was their idea about how I should be and act) before I could think about my own.

To begin with I enjoyed the attention I received from being different. During the eight months I lived in Buenos Aires I saw *one* woman on a motorcycle and she turned out to be Australian. But the attention I got was just another way to distract myself from the black matter inside me. It was another escape, a search for a quick fix for a happy life, which led me to feeling more empty than before.

I wanted out. I had extended the lease on my apartment once and had considered doing it again. When I had two weeks left on the lease, I knew I had to leave. My time in Buenos Aires was up.

Again, I had lost myself in the buzz of everyday life. Contrary to my initial strong intentions, during my eight months in Buenos Aires I had torn down the old layers from my life at home as a lawyer, married to another lawyer and living in a big house, but I had unconsciously replaced those layers with new ones. Now, I was the tall, blonde, independent ex-lawyer from Scandinavia who rode a big motorcycle. How cool was that? At the time I thought it was cool but after eight months I knew it was just another empty shell. A fragile image like the one I had left behind and which had nothing to do with who I am.

The physical luggage

Two weeks before my departure I thought about what to bring on my journey. I made a list of things I wanted to buy, got on my bike and set out to find it in Buenos Aires. Despite not having much clue about what to bring, my list contained a large number of items. I had a specific image of what the items should look like, the quality of them and the price I was willing to pay.

Now, Buenos Aires might be a big city of thirteen million people and the capital of Argentina but that doesn't mean you can buy whatever you need online and have it delivered within two business days. There are a lot of things you can't get hold of in Argentina. Ordering them from a company abroad is only a theoretical option due to the organization of the Argentinean customs and postal system. Unless you have the patience of a dead man and a bank account to match that of Bill Gates, it's not feasible to purchase any consumer goods from companies abroad.

I soon discovered that I wasn't going to find what I was looking for in the exact color, make and price. However, instead of lowering my standards for my purchases I decided to make do with the things I had.

On the day of my departure my supposed eight months of preparation in Buenos Aires amounted to the following:

- intermediate Spanish language skills with expert level in slang, tools and motorcycle parts
- large intake of Argentinean wine and beef
- purchase of a six-year-old motorcycle with side cases, a second hand helmet and second hand tank bag
- purchase of a considerable amount of clothing, like skirts, blouses, handbags and high-heeled foot wear
- purchase of stacks of books
- panic shopping two weeks before departure, please see below.

The complete list of what I decided to take with me looked like this:

- telephone number of the owner of Motocare
- duct tape (purchased in Buenos Aires)
- pink Chanel lip gloss (brought with me from Denmark)
- white Mac Book (borrowed from my dad)
- cell phone (purchased in Buenos Aires) which turned out to be useless since

ninety-five percent of the time I rode in areas without coverage. After four months on the road the phone drowned in the inner pocket of my motorcycle jacket during a ride in heavy rain.

- tent (borrowed from an English rider who rented a bike at Motocare)
- sleeping bag (borrowed from one of the guys in Motocare)
- inflatable mattress (Christmas present from one of my brothers and my sister-in-law)
- camping head light with two extra batteries (same)
- three t-shirts, two tank tops and a wind breaker (purchased in Buenos Aires)
- a pair of summer motorcycle pants (present from my parents)
- a pair of pants for trekking (purchased in Buenos Aires)
- a pair of jeans (brought with me from Denmark) which were now too small due to above-mentioned intake of Argentinean wine and beef. I planned to shed the extra pounds once I left Buenos Aires but things didn't go according to plan. Still, I kept the jeans with me. If nothing else they would remind me of the fact that my butt had gotten wider. I gained a couple of pounds extra on the trip but it wasn't until I had trouble fitting into my only pair of riding pants that I lost the extra weight.

- pink skirt (brought with me from Denmark)
- summer dress (purchased in Buenos Aires)
- unsexy underwear (white granny style) and socks (brought with me from Denmark)
- small towel (purchased in Buenos Aires)
- essential toiletries such as toothbrush, toothpaste, shower gel, shampoo etc.
- a pair of trekking boots (purchased in Buenos Aires)
- a pair of running shoes and a pair of flip-flops (purchased in Buenos Aires)
- motorcycle jacket (borrowed from an Argentinean girlfriend). Unfortunately, the jacket didn't have a liner and was therefore unsuitable for cold weather.
- back protector (present from my parents)
- a pair of summer motorcycle gloves (present from my parents)
- a couple of spare parts like a spark plug, clutch cable, brake pads, air and oil filter (purchased in Buenos Aires)
- chain lubricant (purchased in Buenos Aires)
- tire repair spray (purchased in Buenos Aires)
- pink log book for motorcycle maintenance
- a considerable amount of books (purchased in Buenos Aires). I packed the books in a backpack, which I tied onto the back of the seat of my motorcycle (these were the days before

iPad and Kindle). Before I left Buenos Aires I made a list, which I entitled "Mobile Library", of the books I brought with me. I've just had a look at it and can inform you that I brought thirteen books with me.

I got hold of another eleven books while I was on the road. The reason I know the exact number of books I added to the Mobile Library is that I kept the list updated with the new titles. To distinguish the books I had brought with me from the beginning and the books I added to the library, I wrote an "o' in brackets, like this (o), with an explanatory note decoding the sign to "Intercepted or purchased books" (the "o" stands for the Danish word "opsnappet", which means intercepted).

To finish off the list I added a final section of titles I wanted to get hold of, a section I called: "Interesting titles that are allowed to be intercepted". This list contained another sixteen titles, one of them being Tolstoy's "Anna Karenina" (a book which in the most common editions contains more than 800 pages) as well as the names of four painters I wanted to read about.

In my defense I want to add that I did in fact part with the books once I had read them but after a year on the road I still carried around six or seven books.

What I failed to bring was:

- maps

- GPS
- personal GPS tracking device
- rain gear
- winter clothing
- motorcycle boots
- any clue about what lay ahead.

Looking at the list you don't have to know what a motorcycle is to realize that the content of my luggage wasn't ideal for a motorcycle trip. Yet with this luggage, on a boiling hot mid-December day at noon I began my journey and was stuck in heavy midday traffic. I had planned to leave early to avoid the heat and traffic but ended up spending the morning of my departure riding around Buenos Aires looking for a decent road map of Argentina – an attempt that turned out to be futile. However, there was nothing that could wipe the smile off my face as I sat on my heavy loaded bike, sweating my butt off and breathing in one hundred percent carbon dioxide as I embarked on the biggest adventure of my life.

Admittedly, it was a nuisance to carry around a mobile library but since my motorcycle carried the load 99.9 percent of the time, I was able to deal with it. And to be honest, I would rather have carried this amount of books (and more) could I only have left my mental luggage behind. It was my mental luggage that time after time almost did me in.

One of the many incidents dealing with excess mental luggage happened in southern Brazil when I needed a new chain for my bike.

In Curritiba I found a BMW motorcycle store and stocked up on supplies. I bought thick thermo underwear and rain pants (which turned out not to be waterproof), I got a new air and oil filter but, as chance would have it, they were out of chains for my bike. I couldn't believe it. Here I was, in the biggest BMW motorcycle store I had ever been to, and they didn't have my chain in stock. I asked several times if they were sure, if they had looked everywhere, but I kept getting the same answer: not in stock. Just before I left the store I asked one last time and then I got a yes.

It surprised me that they had suddenly found a chain but I didn't think much of it. It wasn't until I was back in Argentina and a mechanic had taken my bike apart to mount the closed chain that I realized it was too short. It had cost me 100 bucks. I was furious. At this point it escaped my short-term memory that they had tried to tell me they didn't have my chain in stock and that I had been unwilling to listen. I called the store and made a complaint but it was falling on deaf ears.

Instead of getting rid of the useless chain I decided to carry it with me (I found a place for it in my Mobile Library) and wrote an email to BMW Motorrad in Germany with my complaint. Even today, it's a mystery to me how I forgot to press "Send".

By the time I got to Bolivia two weeks later I still carried the chain with me, getting annoyed about the incident in Curitiba every time I felt its heavy presence in my backpack. I told the story about the chain to two Belgian riders I met on the road without getting any sympathy from them. What I got was this: "Why the hell do you carry that thing around with you? Get rid of it! It's only reminding you of the fact that you've been screwed. Why would you want to be reminded of that?"

That did the trick – well, kind of. I sent the chain back to Denmark from La Paz in Bolivia and pressed "Send" on the e-mail to BMW Motorrad in Germany who responded immediately. Then I left it at that and didn't think about the matter until I returned to Denmark six months later. It took me another year to get rid of the chain. I couldn't be bothered to follow up on my complaint to BMW Motorrad now I had left it so long to respond. I ended up giving the chain to a BMW motorcycle store in Denmark who didn't even want it.

So how do you deal with excess luggage – both the mental and the physical? From experience I know what it's about, I've read about it in well-intended self-help books and over the years it's what I have reminded myself of: let go.

Well, thank you Einstein & Co. That's really deep but don't you think I would have let go if I knew how? What does it mean to let go? How do I do it? Whatever I've tried to let go of has stuck to me like super glue. It's haunted me no matter where I've been on the planet and believe me – I've tried so hard to let go that I could make not only my own eyes bleed but yours too. It doesn't work!

Let me illustrate this with an example. When I met the half South American man in Berlin, it left an impression on me that I clung to for years – to be precise: five full years. He was always in the back of my mind as the potential Mr. Perfect for me. Over the years, we kept in contact and from the beginning he was honest with me. Putting it in black and white, he wrote to me: "You're not the woman for me."

I'm sure most of you will agree with me that it's a clear hint. Did I get the message? No. I knew I needed to let go of him and I tried everything. I tried writing about him in my diary, I told myself I shouldn't be thinking about him, that I was wrong to be attracted to him, I told myself that I was treating myself badly for not letting go, I told myself that he was no good anyway, I tried not to be in contact with him for periods of time and despite all my efforts, he remained fixed in my mind as the right man for me.

What worked in the end? I stopped trying to let go. When I stopped trying to let go of him, I let go of him without any effort. After five years I realized that I might have him stuck in my brain for the rest of my life so I thought I might as well get along with my freeloading lodger on the top floor and be honest with him. The first thing I did was write the physical version of this man (who had little resemblance with the man in my mind) an email, explaining the truth. I wrote:

"Ever since the first time we met five years ago (REALLY – all five years!) I've made you a part of my unconscious game, using manipulation and control to get you to love me. When you didn't take the bait, I've blamed you for being unloving, when in reality it was me who was unloving towards you. If we stay in contact, I can't promise you that it won't ever happen again. There are no guarantees in life but I believe that this is the first step to avoid it happening again."

I didn't care if the truth would make him think ill of me or if he didn't want to be in contact with me again. I wasn't being honest to please him, to get him to like me. I didn't even tell the truth "to let go" or with any other gain in mind. I did it to harmonize what went on inside me with what I expressed. Full stop. For years I had either pretended to be soooo over him or pretended to really care about him when in fact I didn't even listen. I brought the pretending to an end.

The day after I had sent the email something strange happened. I realized that despite my unkind behavior towards him I did love him and that it was my attempt to repress my love that had turned me against him and against myself. In that moment I knew I didn't want to die without having told him how I felt. It sounds dramatic but it wasn't. It had nothing to do with him. I didn't want to live with myself if I didn't allow myself to express the love inside me. Whether he returned my love was irrelevant. I realized that loving someone doesn't mean I have to live with that person or be a part of that person's life. So I wrote to him again and told him what I had wanted to tell him since the first time we met:

"I've suddenly realized that I did love you and I still do love you! And there is absolutely nothing you can do or not do to change that. Neither can I.

WOW.

I think I'll just try and write that again. I love you! Ha ha - that feels pretty damn good to let that out! I've actually loved you from the first moment I laid eyes on you."

With that out of the way, my thoughts about him lost their grip. I didn't tell myself that I had to stop thinking about him. If a thought about him entered my mind, I welcomed it, instead of fighting it. It was game over. I had nothing to hide and no image to protect. Over the following six months my attachment to the idea of him disappeared of its own accord. I had finally allowed myself to love him and I knew it didn't mean I had to be a part of his life. I never even needed to verbalize this love. It just is. It's that intimate.

The big joke, I see now, is that letting go is easy. It's the attachment and clinging that requires effort. Once I clearly see the mechanics of my attachments letting go is as natural as exhaling.

The object of the attachment is irrelevant. The workings in play are the same whether I'm trying to give up a bad habit like smoking, trying to let go of an infatuation with a former lover or a resentment towards someone in my current life situation or in my past.

The difficult part – and this is the key – is to stop deriving my sense of self through my thoughts – both positive (I'm great!) and negative (Poor me!). There is nothing wrong with thoughts but when I seek a sense of self or any form of fulfillment (happiness, joy, peace or love) through my thoughts I will never find it. I'm stuck in my identification with the endless loop of alternating states between pain and pleasure.

After my encounter with the man in Berlin, in my mind I kept replaying the joy and bliss I had experienced when we were together. It was my antidote to the emotional turmoil I experienced during my divorce. Initially, it seemed to work. It diverted my attention from my open wounds and it led me to believe that this man was the answer to my problems.

When the replay of bliss lost its effect I replaced it with negative thoughts about him. Now, he was the reason for my troubles. So it went on – back and forth for years.

By the time I wrote to him it had become more painful to hold on to the idea of him (both the positive and the negative) than to face the dark matter I had tried to escape through excessive mind activity. I was willing to fully experience the rejection, to defenselessly experience the emotions and sensations I feared would overpower me if I gave them space. It was a willingness to face the deep-seated, unarticulated fear of being nothing, which had been my faithful companion for years.

In this willingness I experientially understood that the void wasn't real, that I had been trying to escape an illusion. What a laugh! By directly experiencing the emotions and sensations I feared without telling myself a story about what they meant and who or what had caused them I saw their insubstantiality, their nothingness. And gracefully this seeing revealed a deep peace beneath the emotional turmoil.

The unveiling of this peace doesn't mean I won't get my heart broken again – that I won't feel upset or sad. The difference is that now these emotions don't stick to me and drag me down. They don't define who I am.

ON THE ROAD

Vulnerability and strength

Day 230 – July 31, 2007. Puerto López, Ecuador

I can't say I slept well. The fishermen partied all night. I woke up several times because of loud party music.

I had a wonderful day. I went on a whale-excursion boat trip and to Isla de la Plata. From the boat I saw both killer whales and dolphins. It was spectacular. I felt great joy and surprise. And I felt small. I was so impressed by the killer whales, these huge and wonderful creatures and their amazing abilities. I watched them jump and felt grateful that I was allowed to experience it. I also watched a group of dolphins jumping. They swam close to the boat. I looooove whales and dolphins. They're very cute and very clever, though I'm pretty sure I would be able to win a game of chess against them.

I spent three hours walking on Isla de la Plata watching weird birds. Some had blue duck feet. They looked funny because the feet were bulky and big and the owners of the feet had trouble walking. When they stood still their feet overlapped. However, as soon at the birds took off they transformed themselves into elegant, sleek creatures.

I watched the ducks with the blue feet in a fight. A single male got too close to a duck couple and "the husband" attacked the unwelcomed bird. I couldn't help thinking how these birds had no other choice than live out their programming. Most people live the same way – myself included.

I also saw another weird bird. The male had a red inflatable "bag" under its beak. When the male wanted to attract a female he expanded the bag. It looked like a red balloon. It seemed a bit silly but apparently it worked.

The boat ride back to Puerto López was no fun. The waves were big and the boat rocked hard. I didn't feel well and I was relieved to have firm ground under my feet again. On the boat I chatted with a Spanish-Ecuadorian couple and they invited me to join them for dinner together with an American guy and a French guy.

Back at my hotel I jumped in the shower. I was cold and when I turned the warm water faucet, cold water came out. I was not pleased. I breathed in and let the cold beams of water cover my body. A moment later the cold water gave way to hot. It was heaven.

The dinner in the evening was pleasant. Unfortunately, I felt a strong need to let everyone know that I was traveling solo with my motorcycle. This isn't one of my charming habits. Sometimes I feel I need to prove something, because I feel I'm not good enough as I am. It's a shame because without exception the attempt to make myself noticeable or appear as something I'm not is stressful and ugly. I wanted the French guy to notice me. He seemed to take an interest in me on the boat and at the dinner I wanted him to take more interest in me. I wasn't interested in him. I found him arrogant. I just wanted him to give me attention. Because I was so eager to make him notice me the result was the opposite. I guess that's somehow a good thing.

Route planning
Stick to your own business

Most men appear never to have considered what a house is, and are actually though needlessly poor all their lives because they think that they must have such a one as their neighbors have.

Henry David Thoreau

At the beginning of my journey, I woke up with a smile on my face and had to pinch my arm to make sure that it was real: that I was on my way through South America on my dream motorcycle. I was free to go wherever I liked, to do whatever I wanted. I felt I had left behind the internal chaos I experienced during my time in Buenos Aires and I was determined to let approval seeking be the last thing on my mind. From now on I was going to be tuned into my internal GPS.

I kept my route planning to a minimum. I knew I wanted to go to the southernmost town in the world, Ushuaia, also called The End of the World. This place had a magical pull on me. I *had* to go there. I was in the process of shedding layers and getting to the bottom of things and where better to do that than at the bottom of the world.

Once I reached Ushuaia I couldn't get farther south by motorcycle so I had to turn around. Where to next? At the end of Route 3, which I had followed on and off since Buenos Aires, I met a sign that read: "Alaska 17.848 km" (10,090 miles). Standing at the bottom of the world I thought to myself – why not ride to the States? I was reluctant to put myself on a tight time schedule and that meant I wouldn't be able to reach Alaska before the winter. Instead I decided to aim for Los Angeles. As I said it out loud to myself for the first time I felt a deep commitment within me to reach my new goal. Los Angeles it was – no matter what.

From day one of my journey the exact route was less of a concern to me. I only planned one day ahead. I would wake up in the morning, look at the map, ask myself where I wanted to go and get on the bike. However, it didn't take long before I realized that my internal GPS wasn't up to date. I knew I had it. It had given me directions on many occasions though I had often ignored them.

My new approach to decision-making was the following. Whenever I had to make a decision I turned my focus to my body and waited for a reply: a reply in the sense of a bodily sensation, which either felt comfortable or uncomfortable. Comfortable meant "go", uncomfortable was "no-go".

I asked my internal GPS questions like: Where should I go tomorrow? Where should I stay? Should I camp or stay in a hostel? How many nights should I stay? Where should I eat?

I bombarded myself with trivial questions and as a result my internal GPS got overloaded. It wasn't used to this kind of attention and now it had to decide everything from what I ate to where I went to the bathroom.

A few days after I had left Buenos Aires I experienced the first effects of my new approach. I felt confused and lost my sense of direction. The only thing that stayed with me at the beginning of my trip was the magical pull of The End of The World. Sometimes I would sit outside a campground or a hostel and argue with myself whether to go in or not until I got so fed up with myself for not being able to make a decision that I checked-in or moved on just to make something happen.

With this amount of stress related to decision-making, as if my life depended on every move I made, the initial euphoria of living my dream soon wore off. I was so afraid of doing the wrong thing, of making a mistake and not being true to myself that I ended up paralyzing myself. Now, I went in the opposite direction of what I had done in Buenos Aires. If I was in doubt, I was too afraid to make a move and became incapable of making up my mind. I ended up letting chance rule. At the slightest sign of discomfort I was on the move to what I thought would be a better and pleasanter place.

On the first day of my journey I had decided to spend the night in Pinamar but by the time I got to Pinamar it didn't feel like the right place. However, it didn't feel like the wrong place either. It took me more than an hour to choose a campground.

The following day I rode farther south along the coast to Mar del Plata and Miramar but I didn't feel like stopping in either place. I changed course and rode inland. Once I was surrounded by nothing but fields on the Argentinean Pampas the rain started pouring down. There was not even a tree in sight. I didn't have any rain gear so all I could do was continue.

The rain didn't last long but it was so intense that the damage had been done: on my second day of riding I got soaked from top to bottom. An hour later I rode into the town of Necochea, feeling cold and uncomfortable in my wet clothes and determined to stay at the first hotel I saw. Camping was out of the question.

After passing the third hotel, being unable to make a decision, I got the help I needed. A new, heavy downpour was about to start and I had ten seconds to find shelter. I checked into the next hotel.

The following morning I woke up at six o'clock. A bright blue sky greeted me. It was a perfect day for riding. I looked at my map and decided to ride west towards Sierra de la Ventana – a small mountain range I had read about.

I wanted to camp in la Sierra and I had three campgrounds to choose from. I tried to tap into "the wisdom of my body" and feel my way to knowing, which campground was right for me. No answer emerged. My body kept silent. It seemed to say: "Get off my case and stop hassling me with these ridiculous questions". I checked out two of the campgrounds without feeling I had found the right one. Arbitrarily, I chose the third campground.

The campground looked inviting. It had a big lawn and plenty of space to put up a tent and have some privacy. I found a spot for my tent under a tree and started to unpack. First, I had to release my feet from the wet boots. I had used the old trick of having my feet wrapped in plastic bags inside the boots but I can't say I was impressed by the outcome. My feet still got wet and incredible stinky.

As I freed my feet from the temporary gas chamber that the bags had created, I noticed two men across the lawn taking interest in the newly arrived motorcycle rider. And sure enough, by the time I had put up my tent, one of the men gave in to his curiosity and came over to have a chat.

Apparently, he and his friend had wondered why my feet were wrapped in plastic bags. They had presumed it served a higher purpose that in some way would enhance my riding technique. They had also discussed how efficient I looked putting up my tent and had agreed that I must have done it a million times. Rather amused I explained to the impressed Argentinean that the plastic bags had been an attempt to keep my feet dry in my wet boots and that it was the first time in my life I put up a tent on my own. He looked at me in disbelief.

Even though he seemed to accept my explanation I doubt he believed it.

Next morning I considered staying another day but ended up moving on. This time I headed due south towards Patagonia. After a couple of days riding I reached Puerto Madryn on the Atlantic Coast. I sat outside a hostel for twenty minutes before deciding to check in. Christmas Eve was only a couple of days away and I thought it would be nice to celebrate Christmas with other travelers.

After two days in hostel-land I realized that I preferred celebrating Christmas alone. If I wasn't going to celebrate Christmas with family or friends I felt I might as well celebrate it on my own. On the morning of Christmas Eve I left the hostel to find the perfect Christmas spot for my solitary celebration.

I rode south to the town of Trelew but wasn't remotely tempted to stay there. I continued to nearby Rawson, Playa Union and Gaiman but nor did they feel "right". Late afternoon I returned to Puerto Madryn.

My loop excursion amounted to 150 miles with strong and unpleasant side winds and once back in Puerto Madryn I rode straight to a campground outside town. Admittedly, this place didn't feel "right" either but I was tired and annoyed with myself for being indecisive. The campground was spacious and if nothing else it looked like I would be able to get some peace and quiet.

Most of the sites were empty, which left me spoiled for choice. Not good. I chose a site away from the occupied spaces, unpacked and began to put up my tent. However, the tent had a different agenda. No matter what I did it turned out to be the wrong thing. When I finally succeeded I realized the ground was too hard to get the tent poles in.

It was six o'clock in the evening. I had only had breakfast. I was starving and out of patience with the tent business. I wanted to call my family and wish them "Merry Christmas". I had seen a big sign with "Teléfono" by the entrance of the campground but when I inspected the alleged telephone booth, I found an empty cubicle.

I rode into town to make the call and just before midnight in Denmark I got hold of my family. They made so much noise that I couldn't hear what anyone said. By the sounds of it they were having a food and present orgy. It was wonderful to speak to everyone and hear the excitement in their voices. I thought the phone call would make me homesick but to my surprise it didn't. I realized that I was where I wanted to be and if that meant I couldn't celebrate Christmas with my family, so be it.

Before I went back to the campground I had a beer and a snack to fill the hole in my stomach. I needed the extra strength to cope with the tent. Amazed by what a bit of food could do I returned to the campground with renewed energy and went to the caretaker's office to ask for help. The help he offered took the form of a hammer. I went back to my tent and hammered away on the tent poles. That did the trick. Now I was ready to celebrate Christmas.

I was still hungry but I didn't have anything to eat. The shops in town had closed so my only option was the campground kiosk. A depressing affair, it turned out. The shelves in the store were half empty and by the looks of it most of the edible things on sale weren't the product of something that had been alive at some point. I bought a couple of crackers with ham flavor and a chocolate covered ice cream cone. This year, Christmas Eve would be a feast.

I went back to my tent and dug into my Christmas Eve meal. First, the crackers with artificial ham flavor disappeared into my belly. As I was about to treat myself to my ice cream I dropped it onto the dirt.

It was too late. I had reached a point of no return. I was eating the damn ice cream with or without dirt – in this case with dirt. To finish off the meal I drank lukewarm water I had kept in a plastic bottle for a day or two.

My spirits were high but I was in no mood for further excitement. I dug out Paul Auster's "Timbuktu" from my Mobile Library and started reading. By the time I had twenty pages left I couldn't keep my eyes open and fell asleep.

I didn't get much sleep. As it turned out, the Argentineans celebrate Christmas Eve with an arsenal of fireworks that makes the Millennium New Year's celebration on Times Square look like kids' pranks. The fireworks continued for hours and were taken over by loud foul music from a nearby party until eight o'clock in the morning. Under normal circumstances I would have thought: "if you can't beat them, join them" but my body refused to leave its horizontal position. I stayed in my tent and missed out on what sounded like the party of the century.

On Christmas Day I returned to Gaiman south of Puerto Madryn. Even though it hadn't felt like the right place to celebrate Christmas it was a charming town where I could easily spend a day. Without giving in to my indecisiveness I got a room at the Bed & Breakfast "Hostería Dyffryn Gwyrdd" on Main Street. I knew I only wanted to spend one night in Gaiman and that eased the decision-making process. Ten days later I was still in town.

On the day of my arrival a severe lower back pain hit me and after a night's sleep in a bed, which offered as much sleeping comfort as a barrel, I woke up the following day paralyzed. I could hardly walk and riding a motorcycle was out of the question. I was stuck whether I liked it or not.

My prolonged involuntary stay in Gaiman gave me the opportunity to get to know the town better and even though my range of mobility was limited, I quickly concluded that not much went on in Gaiman. Most of the 6,000 inhabitants were descendents from Welsh settlers and the older generations still spoke Welsh. This explained the weird name of my Bed & Breakfast.

On my first day in Gaiman I walked through town in a light drizzle. It was sultry and I welcomed the rain. By Río Chubut the air was crisp and filled with the smell of Christmas tree. I paid a visit to one of Gaiman's many teahouses and ordered the traditional "té completo".

When it comes to cake eating I'm no amateur. I did my best to get through the masses of cakes that were included in the "té completo" for one person but I found myself defeated. As I left the tea establishment the first sign of the backache emerged together with a tire around my waist in an upgraded dimension. Think tractor tire and you get the general idea.

The following nine days my movements were limited to a stroll up Main Street. I visited every shop in town and my inspection revealed that the retail businesses in Gaiman could be divided into three categories:

- humble-jumble stores offering an assortment of goods of a non-edible nature, including nifty ladies fashion for those who are die-hard supporters of the matron look of the 1950s;
- humble-jumble stores offering an assortment of goods of an edible nature and specializing in gross snacks like crackers with artificial ham flavor;
- humble-jumble stores offering an assortment of goods of a non-edible nature for vehicles and heavy machinery. I found a lot of accessories for tractors – though no tires but I guess I wasn't in need of that anymore.

I didn't spend much money in town. My biggest expense was the DVDs I rented in Gaiman's equivalent of Blockbuster. The selection of movies reflected the tastes of previous times that I had encountered in other stores. It included Basic Instinct, Lethal Weapon and other quality classics.

Besides watching movies on my laptop I started reading Bruce Chatwin's "In Patagonia". Up until this point, by coincidence, I'd followed Chatwin's route though Patagonia. He spent some time in Gaiman too – presumably without a backache.

After a week with my condition deteriorating daily, I gave in and had a taxi take me to the local hospital half a mile down Main Street. The hospital looked like a deserted mental institution from the time of the depression in the 1930s. I walked into the building and found it empty. Minutes later a nurse appeared who showed me to the doctor's room. I explained my condition to the doctor and he sent me away with a handful of pink pills. I had no idea what they were but at this point I didn't care as long as they worked.

It's safe to say that my time in Gaiman passed uneventfully. However, it didn't bother me to be stuck. A welcome side effect of my immobilizing back pain was that it had effectively freed me of my decision-making ritual. I couldn't move so I had to stay put.

As the days passed in Gaiman it became clear to me that I couldn't continue my travels unless I changed my approach to making decisions. The indecisiveness had made me miserable. I felt I had got it all wrong in Buenos Aires by letting myself get off track. I was determined not to go down that road again and this had led me to overanalyze every move I made. I had become incapable of making even small decisions, of committing to even the smallest things.

I made a promise to myself that once I left Gaiman I would make my decisions quickly without worrying about the consequences. Once I made a decision I had to stick with it and make the most of it.

Three days after I had taken the first prescribed dose of pink pills I had entered a New Year and was back on the road. When I woke up on January 1st, the day of my return to Denmark felt much nearer. I didn't have any time to lose. On January 2, I was on my way farther south.

It would be wonderful if I were now able to report that my indecisiveness was gone. This wasn't the case. I had become aware of the problem and that was the first step. My indecision was weaker but the underlying fear of making mistakes and getting off track was still controlling my actions. I had lost confidence in my ability to listen to myself. Could I trust myself after having made such a mess of my life? The answer seemed to be "no" and that left me in a state of shock and horror. If I couldn't trust myself how the hell was I going to live my life now that I knew that I couldn't rely on the outer layers I had built up either?

Whether I liked it or not I only had one option: to continue. If I let my fear of making mistakes take total control of my life I might as well be dead. I continued my journey and by use of pure willpower I reduced my indecisiveness considerably. Ultimately, it didn't solve anything.

Willpower had helped me achieve my goals in the past but I knew only too well that it was no fun. It was hard work and it was unrewarding once I achieved them. In the back of my mind I had always thought that if I could eliminate my problems once and for all *then* all would be well.

Pure willpower would never make me stay on track. No matter where I went I would meet challenges I had to deal with. I was bound to have my weak moments and give in to old habits. I had to learn not to equate making a mistake to "the end of the world". Making a mistake didn't mean that I couldn't trust myself or that I would never get it "right" – quite the contrary. When I made a mistake it meant that I had allowed myself to take action and see where that would lead. If I didn't get the result I wanted then in reality I had come one step closer to finding my path. I could rule out one way of proceeding and try out others.

So far, so good. But that didn't explain why I continued to battle with the fear of making mistakes. Why couldn't I just make a mistake, learn from it and move on? In hindsight I realize that I wasn't paying attention to what was happening. Instead of reaping the insight of any given mistake I was more concerned about what other people would think of me if they knew what was *really* going on, if they knew how "hopeless" I *really* was. Ultimately, my fear of making mistakes had nothing to do with not getting it right the first time but was a fear of other people's disapproval. I was faced with my innate fear of rejection.

The more concerned I was about other people's opinions the more lost I got and the more impossible it seemed to respond appropriately to a challenge. It was quite simple. When I worried about what other people thought of me or I was trying to make a certain impression on them (that I was in control of my life, that I was beautiful and smart or whatever happened to be the day's agenda), who was present to run my life? Nobody. And I wondered why I got lost and made the same mistakes over and over again.

Whenever I stuck to my own business, it didn't only free up an enormous amount of resources within me. It also empowered me to take appropriate action. It meant that my focus was on the actions I *could* take. What actions were they? My own. The less time I spent thinking about what others should or shouldn't think or do, the more empowered I became.

It was my strong tendency to be image conscious and approval seeking that had gotten me into trouble time after time. To put it bluntly, I preferred being a phony instead of risking a rejection by standing up for myself.

That's how I ended up studying law. I thought that with a law degree I would be able to earn good money and have the status that went along with it. This way I would be good enough – not in my eyes but in the eyes of other people. I would be accepted and respected. And with the approval of others I thought I had laid the foundation for a good chunk of happiness in life.

The urge to seek approval through money and status partly came from the fact that I grew up in a wealthy area though my parents weren't wealthy. Many of my girlfriends at primary school came from families with lots of money and growing up I felt I couldn't keep up with them. I wasn't one of the pretty, popular girls that all the boys liked either. I was tubby and as far back as I can remember I had a feeling of not being beautiful enough. I was a late bloomer and during my teen years I internalized the belief that I was the kind of girl none of the boys were ever going to like.

I didn't enjoy law school but it never occurred to me to drop out. No, I was going to finish what I had started and once I had my degree *then* I could allow myself to think about what I wanted to do with my life. However, once I finished law school I was busy getting a good job and making my résumé look better for the next one.

Nevertheless, law school did serve an important purpose. It gave me an alibi. If I failed I could always say: "Well, I never liked law anyway and I didn't really try so it doesn't mean anything." If I went for what I really wanted and believed in and I failed, who would I be? If I couldn't cope doing what I really wanted to do, wouldn't I be lost? I was too afraid to find out, so I stuck with law. It was a safe bet.

It took seven years from the time I left law school until I made the jump and followed my passion. Was it because my courage had grown in the meantime? No. I had just become sufficiently fed up with approval seeking, experiencing time and time again that it didn't get me anywhere I wanted to go. Unconsciously, the belief that I would be able to compensate for not feeling beautiful enough or good enough through achievements or possessions had controlled my entire life. Yet no matter what I achieved these feelings of incompleteness and inferiority never left me. When I left my legal career it was with the realization that I wasn't going to be liked by everybody no matter what I did. So for the first time in my life, I stuck to my own business and I did what felt right to me.

For me this step marked the beginning of allowing others to see me as I am (which they do anyway – the only one I've been trying to fool was myself) and of discovering that my sense of worth can't be found outside myself.

It's so simple, it's ridiculous and yet it seems difficult: to stick to my own business. The difficulty lies in the fact that it requires giving up control – or more precisely giving up the idea that I'm in control.

The reality is that I'm not in control. Do I choose my thoughts and emotions or do they arise without any doing on my part? Can I know with certainty what effect my actions have or how they impact others? Can I know without doubt what another person is going through?

It's my experience that even though I would often like to believe that I'm in control, it's not the case. Thoughts and emotions arise out of nothing and if given space they disappear into the same nothingness they came from. My actions more often than not lead to unexpected outcomes (both wanted and unwanted) and I'm often baffled when discovering how people interpret what I say and do.

I've noticed that my frequent attempts to impress people or to leave them with a particular image of me are pointless if not plain counterproductive. People think what they think and ultimately it's got nothing to do with me. Just like me, they interpret what other people say and do based on their past experiences and their conditioning. All we meet is our own projections.

When I believe my thoughts about what other people think or shouldn't think, do or shouldn't do and they don't correspond with reality, I suffer. It's not my business. My business is solely how *I* respond to my surroundings. When my response is authentic I act without hidden motives or attempts to control or manipulate others. I speak my truth and act accordingly.

This doesn't mean that I give air to pent up resentment and have no regard for other people's feelings. What I do to others, I do to myself. Blaming or accusing others of wrongdoing or wanting revenge has nothing to do with responding authentically. These responses carry the weight of past suffering into the present. An authentic response doesn't mean I forget what happened in the past but it means that my present response is not fueled or tainted with the negative emotions that were triggered by past events.

It's only when I stick to my own business, when I listen to my inner voice without giving approval seeking any thought, that I experience a sense of belonging and a clarity on how to proceed.

When I stick to my own business my true worth is revealed. It is revealed beyond concepts in my "beingness" – the same "being" that I share with everyone else on this earth and which is the foundation of true connection between me and others – with or without their approval of me.

An authentic response holds an invitation to others to respond authentically too. But whether my invitation is accepted or not is none of my business.

Day 197 – June 28, 2007. Cochabamba, Bolivia

The ride to Potosí consisted of 125 miles of dirt road and 30 miles of paved road. It was a lovely ride without being particularly exciting. After having spent five days with two Belgian riders I had to get used to being alone. I missed the company but somehow I was happy to be on my own.

When I arrived in Potosí I coincidentally rode straight to my hostel without having the address or a map of town. Crazy stuff.

Potosí lies at 14,000 feet, which means it's pretty chilly – especially at night. However, it wasn't as cold as I had feared. I didn't even need to sleep with my sleeping bag under the blankets.

On my second day in Potosí I went on a guided tour to the old silver mine where they now extract tin. It was a shocking experience. The work conditions were so atrocious that I could hardly believe my own eyes. It was horrible. I spent an hour inside the mine and was relieved to get out again.

Back at the hostel I met two young girls from England with whom I decided to visit Ojo del Inca – a natural hot spring formed as a perfect circle 170 feet across.

When we arrived at Ojo del Inca the park keeper told us that the hot spring was 820 feet deep. I'm not sure I believed him. Nevertheless this piece of information had the effect that we were pretty scared to jump in. We couldn't see the bottom and I have to say that the hot spring did look a bit suspicious. It looked like the perfect spot for the Loch Ness monster. We probably spent ten minutes building up the courage to take a dip without succeeding. Not until the park keeper equipped us with swimming rings did we manage to get in. Pathetic.

Riding techniques
Engage fully

Most people don't want to swim before they know how to.

Novalis

A welcome though mostly unpleasant side effect of my year alone with my motorcycle was the exposure of the way I responded to challenges. Being faced with a daily and constant bombardment of challenges and uncertainty I was able to collect an impressive amount of field material, which revealed a particular pattern.

I'm deliberately not talking about failure and success because I came to understand that when I categorized an event as a failure or success I was labeling it, which prevented me from seeing what was actually happening. Within every success lies its opposite and vice versa. The universal play of duality is inherent in all events. It's not only impossible to say whether an event is good or bad seen from a human being's limited perspective, it's irrelevant when it comes to finding a way to deal with it.

After three months' rumbling around Patagonia, one of the most desolate places on earth, I wondered if I was on the "right" track. I often felt restless and dissatisfied. I thought that if living my dream was this stressful I might as well sit behind a desk in a law firm and get a nice paycheck at the end of each month.

Instead, I had chosen to give up my career and sell my belongings in order to be far away from home and a clean, comfortable bed (which wasn't smelly or occupied by invisible bugs), freezing in the mountains because I hadn't packed any winter clothes (thinking, I'm in *South* America for crying out loud, how cold can it be?) and being scared of crashing and lying around injured. Honestly, you would have thought that someone with a university degree could come up with another way of having the time of her life. As a matter of fact that's exactly what someone with a long education would come up with because we're taught to look for *every* answer outside ourselves.

The fear in me (mainly the fear of crashing, bad dirt roads and rain) was so strong that on the first part of the journey I was rarely free of it. It controlled my life on the road.

My first encounter with dirt happened by accident in northern Patagonia four days after I had left Buenos Aires. I spotted a small dot on my map along with the name "San Blas" on the Atlantic Coast of Argentina and felt drawn to go there. My map showed no other towns nearby. It was an isolated place and was bound to have few inhabitants. What was not to be liked about this place? San Blas was going to be a blast.

I had only missed one aspect in my analysis: the condition of the road getting there. The infrastructure that connects an isolated town in South America is likely to be unsophisticated. Most governments won't feel impelled to spend a fortune building a fabulous road in order to connect 129 people with the rest of civilization. This was the case with the 129 people living in San Blas.

Shortly after I left the paved highway I was faced with the first dirt road of my journey. The road was wide, the dirt was hard, the sun was shining and I was freaking out. At that time, little did I know that this dirt road would appear in any road condition statistics as one of the best dirt roads on the continent.

I thought the dirt would last a couple of miles but by the time I reached San Blas I had covered forty miles on dirt. I had passed two cars on the road. It was early evening and I was terrified of crashing, lying around alone all night.

My worrying thoughts didn't only feel unpleasant in my head. They also had an impact on the rest of my body. It was so tense you could use it as a sledgehammer in an old fashioned steel-forging factory. Not the ideal body composure for riding a motorcycle or undertaking any other activity in the universe except for the above-mentioned conversion to sledgehammer.

By the time I arrived in San Blas both my physical and mental exhaustion was complete. I stayed three days before I was ready to get back on the dirt road. San Blas hadn't been a blast. Surprise. Main Street was a deserted stretch of gravel and all you could do was go fishing. So that's what I did.

As I made my way farther south into Patagonia I encountered more dirt and by the time I reached Tierra del Fuego even the main highway was unpaved. Most of the dirt roads were in what I now know as excellent condition. At the time I had no idea what kind of roads lay ahead and even the sight of a patch of dirt would freak me out.

It took me a while to figure out that the riding technique you use on dirt roads is the opposite of the one you use on paved roads. You lean contrary to the movement of the bike on dirt to create more traction. On paved roads you lean with the bike.

Well, on dirt I was indeed leaning but I was leaning the wrong way. Only on a few occasions did I by accident lean contrary to the movement of the bike. If a rare moment of relaxation sneaked in, my body automatically found the right position, which immediately optimized the performance of my bike and put me in control of it.

After a month on the road I went down the first time. I was riding on the main highway (which was a dirt road) through the Chilean part of Tierra del Fuego. A strong side wind had kicked in. I was on the top of a small hill doing thirty-five miles per hour and as I got to the bottom a strong gust of wind grabbed hold of me. I lost control and a couple of seconds later I was down.

I must have blacked-out because I don't remember the fall itself. Suddenly, I found myself lying in the dirt with my motorcycle on top of me. The engine was still running so I knew that my bike wasn't seriously damaged. I didn't feel any pain and it lead me to conclude that I was okay.

I pulled my left leg out from under the bike, got up and reviewed the scene of the accident.

Location:
- Tierra del Fuego, Chile
- road: dirt
- weather report: windy, sunny, low probability of rain
- traffic alert: no immediate risk of congestion.

The motorcycle:
- left side case transformed to trash
- content of side case now decorating roadside
- left hand guard protector: bent
- gear shifter: bent
- area by rear brake light: bent
- body: tarnished.

The rider:
- left leg: bluish
- stomach: empty
- body: tired and cold
- head: empty and unconcerned.

I picked up the content of the trashed side case before the wind scattered it, took a couple of photos and tried to pick up Dakar. He didn't move an inch. I looked at my watch. It was six o'clock in the evening. I hadn't seen a vehicle for half an hour and I wondered how long I had to wait before someone would come by.

To my surprise I was as calm as the bottom of a deep lake. What I had feared the most had happened. Up to this point every minute I had spent on dirt had been a minute spent in merciless fear.

Now, my biggest fear was reality. I was literally in the middle of nowhere, my motorcycle was down, I couldn't get it up on my own and it didn't bother me. I got some water and bread out of my tank bag, took a rest and looked for a level space to put up my tent in case I had to stay the night. Vehicles are rare on the Patagonian roads, so rare that when you see one you flash the high beam to say hello.

Four minutes later a big truck came by. I waved it to a stop and a fat Chilean truck driver appeared. One look at his clothes gave a whole new dimension to the concept of "dirty". My motorcycle pants, which I feared would soon be able to walk by themselves, had a long way to go.

Together we picked up Dakar and with a screwdriver the truck driver dismantled the remains of my left side case that had refused to let go. Half an hour later I had rearranged my luggage, now with my sleeping bag and inflatable mattress tied onto my backpack, and was ready to twist the throttle. The only thing I had to leave behind was the trashed side case. It was beyond repair but if it hadn't been for the side case my left leg would have looked quite different after the crash. I felt strangely relieved that I was able to leave the side case behind. It had hung too close to the exhaust pipe and the heat from the pipe made the plastic on the case melt. Now, I was rid of that concern.

Five and a half hours after the crash I arrived in the nearest town of Rio Gallegos in Argentina. It was almost midnight. It was pitch black and every hotel in town seemed to be fully occupied. I couldn't figure out why so many people wanted to visit Rio Gallegos. In my opinion there wasn't much to see or do here. The main thing the town had going for it was being the largest town with 100,000 inhabitants nearest Tierra del Fuego and Ushuaia at the End of the World. It was home to a big naval base, which was last in full-blown operation during The Falklands War. The only reminders of the war were the numerous signs scattered around town, which read: "Las Malvinas son Argentinas" (The Falklands belong to Argentina).

Circling the streets of Rio Gallegos at midnight wasn't what I had hoped for after spending twelve hours on the road and having had my first crash on my motorcycle. It took me half an hour's hotel hunting before I found one with a vacant room. It was one of the most expensive hotels in town. A single room including breakfast buffet cost thirty bucks, which was an outrageous price in this part of the world.

Instead of immediately checking in I wondered if it wasn't a bit too expensive. Two minutes later I was back on the bike continuing my search. However, after passing the first fully occupied hotel I woke up, realizing the madness of wanting to save twenty bucks when I was more dead than alive.

I returned to the "expensive" hotel and when I entered the spacious and, for my standards, luxurious room I felt I had arrived in heaven. I slept like a log in the big, clean bed and it wasn't until the next morning it finally hit me, how lucky I had been in the crash. The exhaustion, both physically and mentally, from the crash and the long ride surfaced. I sat in bed crying for no apparent reason. I felt powerless and vulnerable.

I was unable to leave the room. Everything on the other side of the door was overwhelming. I didn't even make it to the restaurant for breakfast. At check-out time I forced myself to go down to the lobby and extend my stay. I got a room for one more night. The following night they had no vacancies.

It escapes my memory what I did in the hotel room that day and a half. I cried and I was scared – that much I do remember. I have just consulted the diary I kept on my journey and it reveals nothing. I made a note that I had a crash and that I wanted to find a place to stay for three or four days where I would be able to relax and read. With the loss of one side case I needed to downsize my Mobile Library. I couldn't get rid of any books before I had read them. That was against library rules. My only remark in my diary about my stay at the hotel was: "I spent two nights in the hotel." The rest of the entry from that day and a half is an elaborate analysis of my unsuccessful attempt to let go of the mental image of the man I met in Berlin two and a half years earlier and a couple of scribbles about an urgent need to lose weight.

After two nights in Rio Gallegos I reluctantly got back on the bike. I didn't get far. In fact I didn't even get out of town before I realized that I wasn't ready to ride. In the depressing outskirts of Rio Gallegos I checked into a hostel close to the highway.

An old lady showed me to the back of the building to a room of about 100 square feet with two bunk beds each containing three beds. I was the first to arrive and I picked the top bed in the corner. It seemed like the best choice for a bit of privacy when the room filled up. However, during the night I realized that the so-called privacy came at a high price. The gas-heating oven had been turned up to maximum capacity and the heat gathered in my top corner of the room. I could hardly breathe and had trouble falling asleep. As I woke up in the morning I felt like I had been run over by a truck. I was in a bad mood and I was upset. I had cried during the night without knowing why.

There was no way I was going to spend another night in the depressing heat chamber. Despite an overhanging risk of total collapse I got back on the bike and rode west.

This day the wind was even stronger than the day of my crash and after twenty miles I had to give up. Several times I was close to being blown off the bike even though I kept my speed to twenty miles per hour. I stopped at a police roadblock and asked an officer if any hotels were nearby. He answered that Hotel Güer Aike was a mile farther down the road. I couldn't believe my luck.

I spent three uneventful days in the hotel as the only guest before I had gained enough strength to continue my journey. I rode west on Route 40, which was surfaced until El Calafate. North of El Calafate I was back on dirt.

Gradually, I began to relax on dirt. The dirt on Route 40 seemed endless anyway, so I thought I might as well learn to cope. For the most part the road was in good condition but when I made it into the southern part of Patagonia in Chile, I got a taste of what a real badass dirt road felt like.

I had entered Chile by Paso Roballos and rode south on La Carretera Austral, the only highway in southern Chile. The dirt was loose and deep, the boulders were generously spread out onto the road and I encountered holes that were capable of swallowing a bus without burping. With two thin wheels and no knobby tires, it wasn't an ideal place to ride for an inexperienced solo rider.

The weather wasn't in my favor either. Clouds coming in from The Pacific dumped their humidity once they met the Andes. It was rainy and cold and I was petrified of having another crash.

I sometimes found myself riding in the footsteps of a grader rake, which left the gravel even looser and deeper and helped big buried rocks resurface. The road was too narrow to allow me to pass the grader rake. To pull over wouldn't help. The road would still be in bad condition and by wasting time in dryish weather without advancing I was increasing the risk of getting caught in a downpour. A downpour would convert the road into a mud bath in minutes and if there was anything I was terrified of (on top of all the other things I worried about), it was mud.

It was an absurd situation because I was surrounded by the most enchanting landscape. When I look back on my journey I'm inclined to say that this stretch of road from Caleta Tortel to El Chaitén offered the most spectacular scenery on the entire journey and for an experienced rider the most superb dirt riding experience. However, most of the time I spent on La Carretera Austral I was too absorbed in my worries to truly appreciate it.

I spent two weeks riding in these conditions and I rarely got out of the firm grip of my fear. It grew in strength and being forced to push myself over my own limits day after day was taking its toll. I seemed incapable of turning things around.

One day I had had enough. I was in Puerto Cisnes, a village along La Carretera Austral, where I had spent three days. On the morning of my departure I knew that the faucets of the sky would be wide open. I looked at the dark clouds, thinking about the many miles of challenging dirt road ahead, but instead of letting the fear surface I said out loud – I guess directed aimlessly at the universe: "You can rain all you want and you can give me the worst dirt roads and I might go totally down but I'm gonna go and I'm gonna have a great time. It's not up for discussion. Take it or leave it."

I loaded the bike, got in the saddle and twisted the throttle hard. Soon after, it began pouring down. I was soaked, the dirt road was mean and I didn't give a damn. I had a wonderful time. I felt at one with my bike. I relaxed my body, kept my focus and let my bike do what it had been designed to do. I didn't interfere.

It was as if I had hit a switch, which completely changed my world – not because of a change in my outer circumstances but because of a shift within me. Instead of holding myself back in the merciless grip of my fear I gave everything I had. I put everything on the line, my whole existence without reservations, accepting whatever was coming my way and trusting that I would be alive and okay at the end of the day. I became at one with my surroundings and effortlessly I made my way forward with high intensity, knowing I was safe.

This shift made me realize that during my first three months on the road I had unconsciously developed a number of different riding styles. To be exact, I had five riding styles.

My five riding styles were:

Couch Riding
Description: Passive and laidback riding. The rider is inattentive and bored and her butt is deep in the seat. The rider has a strong tendency to lean backwards as if she was sitting at home on her couch. The couch position does nothing for her ability to handle the bike.

Use: The rider is tired or a lazy-lay-about.

Level of joy (on a scale from 0 – 10): Four. Five if you have a particularly big butt due to the fact that most of the energy is concentrated in that area of the body. Being a couch potato on a motorcycle isn't an uncomfortable experience. It's just hopelessly dull.

Resistance Riding
Description: Unwillingness to adapt to present road and weather conditions. The rider believes that if she stubbornly resists the conditions they won't persist. The concept of "acceptance" is a fruit from another galaxy. The rider is experiencing an overwhelming internal time pressure despite not being on a schedule.

Use: The rider is in a rush for no reason and wants the ride over with.

Level of joy: Very close to zero. Glimpses of relaxation can accidentally sneak in (in practice it's amazingly hard to stay in total resistance mode a hundred percent of the time) and that's why I haven't rated the level of joy of this riding style as absolute zero.

Panic Riding
Description: Stressful, fearful and unbalanced riding. The rider is carefully listening to the fearful voices in her head and is imagining everything that could go wrong. The rider is tense, unfocused and feels she's in acute danger even though there is none.

Use: The rider is feeling victimized (by thoughts in her head though she doesn't realize that the pain is self-created) and helpless and has no interest in finding a solution. Momentary motto: "Why be happy when you can be crappy".

Level of joy: A big fat zero.

Engaged Riding
Description: Active and dynamic riding. The rider is one hundred percent alert. She is engaging fully and is in tune with the bike. Speed is maximized under the present road and weather conditions. She's going beyond her comfort-zone without losing her inner peace. She's filled with enthusiasm.

Use: The rider is present in the Now and is improving her riding skills.

Level of joy: Two gorgeous handfuls.

Flow Riding

Description: Active and balanced riding. The rider is alert and her body follows the movements of the bike. She is calm and in a natural flow with her bike and the surroundings. The speed isn't maximized. It's perfectly adjusted to the present road and weather conditions. The rider stays within her comfort-zone.

Use: The rider is alert and calm. She experiences a total lack of stress, inner resistance or pressure to get somewhere.

Level of joy: A big happy ten.

A realistic estimate would conclude that I spent more than seventy-five percent of my time Couch Riding and Resistance Riding with brief sections of Panic Riding thrown in. It took little inattention on my part to end up in these riding styles and once I was there it was hard to shift.

With a few exceptions I would get on the bike and begin the day's ride as a happy camper. My passion for riding a motorcycle had been pent up for so many years that it was impossible to keep it down. During my first year of riding, no matter how low I felt when I opened my eyes in the morning, the sight of my motorcycle cheered me up. I loved riding it and still do.

I would get on the bike with a smile on my face and get into Flow Riding. However, as the day progressed, endless mind activity veiled the joy that poured out of me and gave life to the motorcycle.

Despite my thoughts' plentitude and persistence it was shocking to realize that most of them had a negative connotation. Loops of negative thoughts followed by negative emotions about my past or future took my attention away from enjoying my passion. In essence these thoughts only covered two themes: "I have been wronged" or "I am wrong". From here they led to another thought that began with one of the following: "I need..., I don't need..., I want..., I don't want..., I should..., I shouldn't... I can... and I can't..." The only variables were the persons and situations in which I was wrong or was wronged and the type of lack I gave voice to.

Let me give you an example:

"My friend X hasn't written to me in two weeks."

"She doesn't care about me."

"I need her to write to me."

In response to these thoughts my mind would produce the proof that the thought "she doesn't care about me" was true. My mind would go to the vast memory bank of times when I've felt hurt by people in the past, find an emotion from a similar situation and bring both the emotion and the past situation to the present moment. This way the painful memory would fuel the recent thought and emotion and I would feel justified in my complaint and feeling of lack.

At the time, I was unconscious of these mind patterns. All I was acutely aware of was the emotional suffering I experienced as a consequence. I was riding my dream motorcycle through Latin America, I had no obligations, I had enough money and I had plenty of time, yet I failed to notice it. My mind patterns consumed most of my energy and led me into opposition against the beautiful and magnificent present moment that was a reality at every breath I took.

Once the negative thoughts and emotions gained momentum, there seemed to be no way stopping them, no matter how hard I tried. At the beginning of my journey it was only after more than ten hours on the bike that they left me alone. When I reached a point beyond exhaustion they gave me a rest. Those few moments – when I had burned myself down and my mind went quiet – were without doubt worth all the agonizing hours on the bike in my own company.

As I made my way through Latin America I learned to deal with my mind patterns in ways that didn't involve wearing myself out completely, physically or mentally. The first step was to become aware of the thoughts. When I identified with my thoughts, I was unconscious and there was nothing I could do but act out my conditioned mind patterns. I was a powerless puppet.

Once I became aware, I had a choice. I could indulge in the thoughts or I could break away. To break away I needed to be with my thoughts without judging them, resisting them or trying to change them. Once I gave them space without judging them they would let go of me.

The key, I found, was attention. The thing with attention is: either I pay attention right here and now or I don't. The good news is that I can quickly go from not being attentive to being attentive. In a flicker of a moment I can become aware of my thoughts and emotions and in this awareness I create the possibility of them loosening their grip on me. In this space my riding style cannot avoid being affected even though it doesn't necessarily happen all at once.

The aim of becoming aware of the different riding styles isn't to eliminate the riding styles I don't like. The only result I would get is a strengthening of them. It's not possible to *make* them go away. My mental approach needs to be one of exploration and curiosity. In a sense, these riding styles served a purpose and once that purpose was gone, the riding style went with it. They were a wake up call, giving me the chance to bring my attention into the present moment and allowing me to experience life fully.

During a ride on a curvy paved highway I noticed that I didn't like to lean to the left. It had been a problem since I started riding but I had chosen to ignore it because I didn't know how to deal with it. Whenever I hit a left curve, I was scared and I didn't enjoy the riding experience. Strange, I thought. I know my bike has no preference as to which side I lean. The stress must be coming from me. It annoyed me that I was riding through a beautiful canyon on a curvy highway not enjoying half the experience. After an enjoyable right curve followed a tense left curve.

I decided to observe what I did in a right curve and what I did in a left curve. When I went into a right curve I focused my attention on where I wanted to go (the end of the curve) and then I let the bike do the rest. I didn't try to control the bike or the angle of leaning. I trusted the bike to do what it had been designed to do and went with the flow.

When I hit a left curve I tightened my muscles even before I was in the curve and looked directly in front of the front wheel. I slowed down and I resisted the lean. I didn't relax until I was out of the curve.

Now I knew what worked and what didn't. Without judgment I had observed the differences. All I had to do was to apply my riding technique in right curves, to left curves. How difficult could that be? Very.

The resistance I felt in my body when I focused my attention on the end of a left curve was massive. I felt I was in free fall and that I was going down. It was terrifying. But when I succeeded in applying my right curve technique to left curves I wasn't in doubt of its superiority. Even though I was scared and felt I had no control it was clear to me that I was much safer and that with practice I would be able to enjoy left curves to the same extent as right curves.

Without exception in Flow Riding and Engaged Riding I am experiencing a high degree of awareness and effortlessness. What separates these riding styles from the rest is that I engage in the activity of riding with my whole being without holding anything back. It feels like time has stopped and I'm not growing any older. I'm completely present in the Now. I feel I'm expressing my innermost being, that every movement on the bike is an expression of my essence.

In these moments there is so much space around every move I make that I feel the total impact of them. My mind is quiet and I'm aware of the pure joy of being alive. It's that simple. It's not the activity of riding a motorcycle that is producing this effect. It's the lack of resistance to my surroundings and my mental and emotional state that allows the joy inside me to surface.

To experience life fully I have to engage fully. On countless occasions I've refrained from engaging fully in life because I've been afraid of failing, be it in a new job, meeting new people or meeting a man I really like. I used to feel that if I opened up and didn't hold anything back I would be wiped out if I failed, that I would have no strength left to get up and continue.

I now realize that it's the fact that I'm holding back that is draining my energy and making it seem impossible to move on if I were to fail. When I open up I *do* become vulnerable; however, in that vulnerability lies my greatest strength. If I have engaged fully, if I have given a situation everything I have, what have I got to lose? Nothing. I already gave it. And because I gave it I now have room for receiving the fruits too. I'm able to close the circle. Only with the willingness to be open and vulnerable am I willing and able to love and be loved.

Day 135 – April 28, 2007. Barra da Lageo, Brazil

Under a grey sky I rode north from Punta del Este in Uruguay and mid afternoon I crossed the border into Brazil. It's crazy! I still haven't understood that I'm in Brazil. It's mind-boggling. I never expected I would visit Brazil by motorcycle. I've totally surprised myself. I believe that once in a while it's a healthy thing to do. I can actually recommend that you surprise yourself about once a month. It rocks!

It's wonderful to experience a new country. A lot of weird stuff pops out. To get to know a new country it's always a good idea to begin in the supermarket – following the motto: "You are what you eat" (right now I don't want to know who that makes me out to be – ARGH!).

Anyway – who are the Brazilians? Judging by their supermarkets they're fond of alcohol and hard liquor, cleaning products (very impressive section of cleaners). Bread and cakes are happily eaten and they are mad about exotic, tasty and fresh fruits!

Another thing I've noticed is that you can pay with credit cards in most shops – even using the chip. Hallooow – is that cutting edge or what? Their gas stations are also pretty cool. Never in my life have I seen gas stations this size. You could easily spend days exploring these "cities of fuel". I've had to force myself to keep my visits to less than half an hour but for someone like me with a weak spot for gas stations there are many temptations in Brazil.

Generally, there's less "wild wild west" about Brazil than Argentina. Well, at least here in the southern Germanic part of Brazil. I've seen fewer lethal piles of shit on wheels on the roads and drivers seem to respect some traffic rules. That doesn't apply to the speed limits – at least in comparison to the Argentineans. Neither have I witnessed completely insane and hazardous over-takings – yet.

North of Tramandaí I rode along the Atlantic coast and miles of Brazilian white beaches. The sun was shining from a clear blue sky and Dakar's engine ran smoothly. It was a beautiful ride. Brazil is very exotic. Honestly, I still don't get it that I'm here with my own motorcycle. It's crazy. So many people have warned me about traveling in Brazil by motorcycle – even Brazilians – but somehow I feel at ease in this country.

Keeping warm
Relax

Defense is the first act of war.

Byron Katie

During most of my motorcycle journey I struggled to keep warm. I wore summer riding gear, my motorcycle jacket missed its liner, I didn't have proper rain gear and my sleeping bag, supposedly filled with down, couldn't keep me warm at night.

With this clothing it was hardly a surprise that I froze under attack from a snowstorm in the Andes in southern Argentina. But that I was cold and uncomfortable when it was sixty degrees and sunny didn't seem right.

I had *one* warm night in my tent. It was a night in Sierra de la Ventana in the province of Buenos Aires, Argentina. I had been on the road for three days. It was midsummer and probably eighty degrees during the night. When I woke up in the morning, still in my sleeping bag, the sun had converted my tent from sleeping cubicle to pizza oven. Admittedly, I felt a bit hot but I wasn't uncomfortable.

I often thought fondly about that warm night in my tent as the number of sleepless nights increased due to my inability to keep warm.

Proportionally my frustration increased. The thing was, it wasn't actually that cold. The daytime temperature in most places I rode was in the fifties and sixties and at night the temperature dropped into the forties. But those were the rare cold nights in my tent. Under these circumstances it didn't seem right that I was agonizingly cold.

As I got closer to Tierra del Fuego at the southern tip of South America with next stop being Antarctica, I was still reading Bruce Chatwin's "In Patagonia". By the time I reached Tierra del Fuego so did Chatwin, but he didn't seem to be concerned with the same issues I was.

On his way north from Ushuaia he picked a path, which turned out to cross a river about twenty times. At one point Chatwin fell into the cold river and struggled to get out again. He got soaking wet, yet he continued until nightfall and stopped only when it was too dangerous to continue walking in the dark. He spread out his sleeping bag on a level space and lit a fire. He reports that the sleeping bag was damp and warm but that was nothing compared to what was to come next. Chatwin continued:

"And then I heard the sounds of an engine and sat up. The glare of headlights showed through the trees. I was ten minutes from the road, but too sleepy to care, so I slept. I even slept through a rain storm."

This was just too much. How on earth did Chatwin keep warm at night after having fallen into a cold river, getting soaked and sleeping in his damp sleeping bag during a rainstorm in Tierra del Fuego? This was the mid 1970s for crying out loud, long before high-tech camping gear had been invented. I didn't get it. Okay, he admitted that the next two days he was too stiff to move and did absolutely nothing. Still, I had a hard time accepting that I was freezing in my high-tech sleeping bag and tent at nightly temperatures of fifty degrees. Something didn't add up.

A month later I made it into southern Patagonia in Chile without any change in my ability to keep warm. I was beginning to think that maybe I was built differently than most other human beings. For as long as I could remember I had been struggling to keep warm and not even the warmest clothes seemed to help me.

When I finished Chatwin's book I started reading Thoreau's "Walden" and I found myself consumed by his writing. It certainly didn't get less interesting when Thoreau touched the subject of keeping warm. Thoreau wrote:

"By proper Shelter and Clothing we legitimately retain our own internal heat; but with an excess of these, or of Fuel, that is, with an external heat greater than our own internal, may not cookery properly be said to begin? Darwin, the naturalist, says of the inhabitants of Tierra del Fuego, that while his own party, who were well clothed and sitting close to a fire, were far from too warm, these naked savages, who were farther off, were observed, to his

great surprise, "to be streaming with perspiration undergoing such a roasting.""

He continued:

"Most of the luxuries, and many of the so called comforts of life, are not only not indispensable, but positive hindrances to the elevation of mankind."

This was perhaps taking it one step too far for my liking. I'm very happy with my high-tech camping gear and I have a hard time believing that in and of itself it constitutes a positive hindrance to anything.

From my point of view the biggest hindrance to keeping warm wasn't caused by my camping gear and modern clothes but my resistance to the cold. Excessive clothing could rightfully be seen as an expression of the inner resistance and maybe this is what Thoreau was pointing to.

On the road I had plenty of time to observe my response to cold weather. I would tighten every muscle in my body as if I could make the cold go away by resisting it with pure muscle power.

The strategy didn't work. Even if I had had the muscle mass of Arnold Schwarzenegger, it wouldn't have worked. On the contrary, I felt colder and experienced more agony and exhaustion.

Instead I tried to relax, to let the cold dig into my flesh and bones without resistance. It might sound like an easy thing to do, but I found it almost impossible. I had developed the habit of not only tensing up when exposed to the cold. I also got tense if I thought I might be cold. I believed that I could prepare myself for the cold by tightening my muscles while still warm.

A couple of times my experiment worked. I managed to relax and the result was astounding. I suddenly didn't feel the cold. Don't get me wrong, my body was cold, my hands and feet numb, but the cold didn't get to me. I was cold and that was the end of it. After a while I began to defrost and generate enough heat from the inside to keep my body warm.

It seems to me that it is not the comforts of life, to use Thoreau's words, which are a positive hindrance to keep my body warm but my unwillingness to relax. Ultimately, keeping warm is necessary for the survival of any human being. If my body temperature drops even a couple of degrees it becomes dysfunctional. If I'm warm enough, it also means I'm safe. That's what this business about keeping warm is all about for me. I want to feel safe, not only on a physical level but also on an existential level.

My entire life I've sought security outside myself through acquisition of things or achievements. I spent five and half years at law school because I thought it would lead to a good job, which would provide me with the money and status that would keep me happy and safe. Did it? No. I still felt insecure. So I continued my search. Perhaps marriage would do the trick? If I could get a man to love and appreciate me, then I might feel safe. But no. Once I was married I realized that it didn't change a thing inside myself. Then a big house? Nope. Well, then what? What hadn't I tried? I hadn't tried to follow my *own* dreams. That had to be the answer. So I left my legal career, sold my belongings and embarked on my Latin American motorcycle adventure and still I didn't find any safety.

The only thing left I haven't tried seems to be to have kids but quite frankly I don't believe they will do the trick either. I've met too many miserable people with kids and nothing but worries to make it a plausible solution. Based on my own futile attempts to find security outside myself I've concluded that it cannot be found by adding something to my life. Whenever I add something to my life and base my sense of security on it, like a good job, a big house, a partner or a slimmer body, simultaneously I create the fear of losing it.

Fear is not the problem but the fact that I base my sense of security on something outside myself. How do I deal with this? Is it possible to base a sense of security on something that cannot be lost?

While traveling I tried to isolate myself. I made one phone call on Christmas Eve to my family and one phone call to a girlfriend – that was it. I only communicated via e-mail. I rarely had company on my trip. I sought out isolated places and spent most of my time alone. I believed I would feel safe if I isolated myself from everyone else. This way no one could hurt me.

It was an insane experiment and after my first three months on the road in Patagonia I realized without a shred of doubt that, although I create the reality I experience, it means nothing and makes no sense if I don't relate to others. I can only understand myself and experience myself in relationship.

Okay – so isolation is out of the question. Then what? When I look back on my motorcycle journey I always felt safe when I met my surroundings openly. No matter where I happened to be my best protection was to be disarming. When I was alert and relaxed I felt safe. If there's nothing I'm defending, what is there to be afraid of?

On the day I rode from Bolivia into Peru a general strike had closed down "El Alto", the high plains of Peru. The road from the Bolivian border town Copacabana to Cusco in Peru had been blocked with stones, boulders, trash, bonfires and a carpet of broken glass. People were out in the streets and the atmosphere was tense. Kids threw stones after me and people shouted "gringa". Riots and fights between the army and the demonstrators made the road and each town I passed look like a war zone.

It took me three days to ride the 250 miles from Copacabana to Cusco. The first 100 miles from Copacabana to Juliaca took a day. I arrived in Juliaca late afternoon and, with the help of two bicycling young men I met outside town, I found a cheap hotel. The following day the riots regained strength and the gate to the hotel was locked. No one was allowed to leave.

After two days in the hotel I continued north. People had begun to clean up the mess from the riots. Most of the boulders had been removed but the carpet of broken glass still covered the road. The atmosphere was less tense and people were calmer even though demonstrations were still taking place.

Twice I got caught in a demonstration. The first crowd of about a hundred people came marching towards me, blocking the road. I couldn't get round it so I stopped. When the crowd reached me I sat quietly on my bike and let them pass me. Some people pushed the bike up and down and shouted "gringa" as they passed me.

The second demonstration was smaller and the people seemed less agitated. A couple of men came up to me with a container of red paint. They wanted to write something on my bike and asked for my permission. I told them they could write on my windscreen and ten minutes later I continued my ride with the words "Viva SUTEP" on the screen. I later learned that SUTEP is the teachers' union in Peru.

While I was stuck in the demonstrations I wasn't afraid. I was alert. Once I got to Cusco I did feel worn out. It had been a stressful experience but I never felt unsafe or afraid of people harming me. When I got caught in the first demonstration I thought: "if just one person shouts, "let's get her" then I'm doomed". But I let the thought pass and stayed vigilant and relaxed. I had no chance against them. I was no threat to them. At most I was a nuisance.

I had no idea how to respond so I allowed the situation to be as it was. I didn't try to *do* anything. I didn't attempt to be invisible or to appear calm. I stayed where I was, *as I was*, and let the demonstrators pass me. I refrained from "doing" and mentally opposing the situation. And that's when I noticed that there's a huge difference between facing a hundred demonstrators and facing a hundred demonstrators who want to hurt me. The first is facing reality, the second is dealing with a thought in my mind, which has nothing to do with reality.

An attitude of refraining from mentally opposing situations with other people helped me stay clear of trouble during my entire journey. Even though I spent most of my time alone, attracting plenty of attention to myself by being a solo female motorcycle rider, I never felt threatened by other people.

Once in Colombia I was waiting for a small ferry to cross Río Magdalena. At one point I had ten men standing around Dakar and me. I was the only foreigner and only woman. I felt no threat, just friendly curiosity. A young guy asked me to take of my sunglasses so he could see my blue eyes. I lifted them, he smiled and I put them back on.

Being disarming didn't mean that I left my bike unlocked, didn't keep my purse hidden or refrained from saying "no" to people. Sometimes it's best to turn around and get the hell out of a situation. What I mean is that when I'm disarming I become more sensitive to my surroundings, which allows me to respond appropriately to the challenge I face at any given moment. If I resist, if I tighten my muscles and put up a defensive wall, how am I able to sense what is going on in *this* moment and find the appropriate response?

No two situations are the same and if I act in the same way no matter what the challenge looks like I'm not truly meeting the challenge and thus able to overcome it. Being disarming has nothing to do with passivity – on the contrary. It means that I'm alert and relaxed and it's from this position I take action – if needed. It allows me to experience the freshness of each moment and be in alignment with "what is". In this alignment I'm safe. "What is" – no matter what shape it takes – can't be lost.

Day 24 – January 7, 2007. Rio Gallegos, Argentina

The first thirty miles south of Rada Tilly were pure pleasure. Route 3 weaved its way through the barren landscape along the Atlantic coast. Then it was back to a straight road and its surrounding nothingness, a landscape that had begun to tire me despite its fascinating vastness. However, in the middle of nothing a minor problem occurred.

I'd carefully studied my map and planned to buy gas in the village of Fitz Roy where it indicated the presence of a gas station. Fifteen miles north of Fitz Roy Dakar's low fuel warning light came on (also known as the "oh shit, I need to get gas light"). However, in Fitz Roy all I encountered was a deserted gas station. Not good. I'd covered fifty miles since the last town with a gas station and the next ahead was eighty miles farther south. I probably had gas for another thirty miles.

Behind the old gas station I found a kiosk amongst a couple of deserted houses. I asked at the kiosk if they had any gas for sale. The owner told me that he was sold out but that he would pick up more gas in the afternoon. I'd have to wait five hours, which by Argentinean standards probably would turn into ten.

I left the kiosk disorientated and sat down in the gravel to conceive of a new plan. What now? At this point I was blank – my head, which under normal circumstances teemed with thoughts, was empty. It was a wonderful sensation. Somehow it didn't get to me that I was temporarily stranded in this shady village. The sun was shining and the world seemed trouble-free. I relaxed and let the sun warm up my body.

I've no idea how long I sat there, probably only a short while, but suddenly the owner of the kiosk came up to me and asked me to wait. Err – okay. A minute later he returned with a gallon of gas, which we quickly poured into Dakar. Then I was ready to continue.

Before I set off I decided to lube the chain and that turned out to be a wise decision. When I looked down I caught sight of my credit card lying on the ground. Apparently, it had fallen out of my purse when I paid for the gas. I couldn't believe my luck.

Problem solving
Accept

Most people live in delusion, involved in their problem, trying to solve their problem. But just to live is actually to live in problems. And to solve the problem is to be part of it, to be one with it.

Shunryu Suzuki

Somewhere in the distant past I picked up a particular problem solving approach: the bulldozer approach. It's very simple, you can even teach it to kids though I can't recommend it. When things are not going according to *your* plans, deny what is happening and apply as much force as possible and thus bulldoze the obstacles out of the way – or at least silence them.

It starts with the simple idea that I can make unpleasant things, people or events go away and never return if I pretend they're not there. Whatever I want to accomplish I keep on doing it my way and if I meet resistance, I try harder. It's a full-force, one-speed attack technique (maybe this was why my eldest brother, when we were growing up, told me I would become the first female general in the Danish army).

Trying harder is painful and the more I push, the less I achieve. I'm not only wearing myself out, everyone around me is exhausted too.

The first thirty years of my life my preferred response to challenges was the bulldozer approach. On my thirtieth birthday my husband (at the time) and I had an argument, the outcome of which was my husband's refusal to speak to me. Ten days later he opened his mouth again and told me he had quit his job.

A year earlier we had bought a big house north of Copenhagen and even though I had a decent salary there was no way we were able to pay all our bills with one income.

Up to this point I had no idea how unhappy the man I lived with had become and it wasn't until after our separation when I met the half South American man that I realized how unhappy I had become too.

The man I lived with at the time had his complaints, many of them legitimate, but I never listened. Not even when he quit his job did I stop to listen. Looking back I now see that for months he had been trying to tell me that he wasn't happy but I wanted to hear nothing of it.

The thing was this. If I began to listen to him, it meant I had to start listening to myself too and that was far more scary than listening to him. There was no way I was going to do that. Imagine. What if I realized that I wasn't living the life I wanted to live? What if I had to make a lot of changes? How would I cope? If I had any say, I was going to do whatever it took to avoid it. I believed that if I kept on denying that something was wrong, eventually it would go away.

At this point in my life the most daunting thing I could imagine happening to me was getting divorced (together with public speaking which also made death worth looking forward to). Whether I liked it or not, I *had* to make our marriage work. I was convinced that if I became a divorcee at the age of thirty my life would be over and that no other man would want to be with me. I would be damaged goods forever. Not a good scenario for someone who at that point believed in the concept of romantic love until death us do part.

Despite my efforts to ignore whatever was going on around and inside me, the argument with my husband on my birthday set something in motion I was unable to control. While my husband, who is British, was in England visiting his family, I printed out the separation papers from the municipality's website even though I still thought I was determined to save our marriage. When my husband returned I was happy to see him again and hoped we would be able to work through our problems (which to me meant to pretend they weren't there and get on with the program).

He told me that he had talked to a recruitment consultant in London and upon hearing this I fetched the separation papers and calmly asked him to sign. I had already put my signature down. Without objection he signed.

The following four months we lived together in our big house keeping our communication to an absolute minimum. When the house was finally sold I moved into my four year-old nephew's room until, on New Year's Eve, I sat on a plane on the way to South America for the first time in my life.

My first South America trip was a mind-boggling experience. I had never traveled alone outside Europe except on business. I didn't speak a word of Spanish and I knew nothing about the continent I was about to visit. Yet I was unconcerned. The worst thing I could imagine happening to me had just happened. What could I possibly have to worry about now? I felt I was at the bottom and that there was only one way to go: up.

I spent two months backpacking alone in South America. My new worry-free approach to life was liberating. I went with the flow and, whenever I met a challenge, I didn't resist it but accepted it and found a way through.

The first obstacle came quickly. I hadn't even arrived in South America when things failed to go according to plan. My plane was delayed and in Houston, Texas I missed my connecting flight to Rio de Janeiro. I had twenty-four hours in Houston and it was New Year's Eve.

The airline company got me a room at one of the airport hotels. I dumped my stuff, went to the car rental agency and booked a big American SUV for the following day. Back in my hotel room I opened a bottle of champagne that my sister-in-law had given me (these were the happy days when you were allowed to bring liquids on board an airplane) and jumped into the New Year from the hotel bed while watching a live broadcast from Times Square in New York.

On January 1, I got in the SUV, turned on the satellite radio and drove to the NASA Space Center where I spent a delightful morning. I saw the Mission Control Center that was used when Armstrong took his first step on the Moon and said: "That's one small step for *(a)* man; one giant leap for mankind". The computer they used in Mission Control filled a big room and had a capacity 300 times smaller than a standard laptop in 2005. At the Space Center I also touched a stone from the moon, which was 3,8 billion years old. It put my recent worries into perspective.

After the NASA experience I paid a brief visit to Galveston by the Gulf of Mexico before I returned to the airport. I had had a perfect first day of the new year, which hadn't been part of my plan. And still I made it to South America.

With the bulldozer approach, a day like the one I had in Texas couldn't have happened. I would have been too thrown by the fact that things didn't go according to plan. I would have focused all my energy on resisting the change, unconsciously hoping, or perhaps even expecting, that this pressure would scare the universe, make it rewind time and put things in my preferred order.

This hits the nail right on the head. Why is it I think I know what's best for me even when reality turns out differently? Is it true that from a human perspective (through the mind) I can know with certainty what's best for me in the long run?

My divorce was devastating to me, or to be precise, to the image I had of myself, but it turned out to be one of the best things that had happened to me. The divorce made a cleft in my self-image so deep that it was beyond repair. I knew it was pointless to try to repair it and because of it, I was able to experience how limiting my old self-image had been. It had been a straightjacket and I had voluntarily put it on. It wasn't my husband, my parents, my work or society imposing all the limitations I experienced. I was doing it. Why? Because I didn't know better. I was stuck with the belief that it wasn't okay to be me as I am. I had to be different. To be worthy of love and appreciation I tried to be something I wasn't. This is where the bulldozer approach originates.

The bulldozer approach isn't only applied outwardly. It's applied inwardly too. It's here the pushing and shoving begins: with an unwillingness to respect my natural boundaries – to say "yes" when I mean "no" and "no" when I mean "yes". This has been a recurring theme in my life. With the hidden motivation of gaining someone's approval, I've often refrained from being true to myself and being honest about my feelings.

During my motorcycle journey I met another traveler with whom I fell in love. At one point he started telling me about one of his ex-girlfriends and he frequently returned to the subject. I believed that to get him to like me I needed to show interest in his former girlfriend and throw in a couple of questions to make sure that my interest seemed real.

The more he talked about his ex-girlfriend (who according to this man also happened to be incredibly beautiful) the unhappier I became and the less I wanted to be with him.

I decided to be honest, to tell him about my feelings, that I was beginning to feel unwanted and that I didn't feel like being around him any longer. He was surprised and upset to hear this. He explained that he thought I had been interested in hearing about his former relationship because I'd asked questions about it. But once I'd leveled with him, he stopped talking about his ex-girlfriend and we were able enjoy the remaining time we had together.

I had been unwilling to accept that I didn't want to hear about his ex-girlfriend. I thought I oughtn't to feel uncomfortable about it, that I was uptight and unnecessarily insecure. I judged myself and instead of being honest I distanced myself from him, which at the time was the opposite to what I wanted.

It's my experience that accepting things *as they are* (that is, without judgment) and being honest about them acts like a razor-sharp blade through problems and allows me to become at one with them. It's about accepting not only my outer circumstances but even more so my inner ones – my thoughts and emotions. Would I have had a problem if I hadn't told myself that it was wrong not wanting to hear about the ex-girlfriend of the man I had just fallen in love with? I doubt it. I would have been able to tell him straight away that it bothered me and asked him to stop. If he then kept on talking about her, I had a choice: I could continue listening (either feeling bad about it or learning to deal with it) or I could stop spending time with him. Where's the problem? There isn't one.

The only way a problem could creep in would be if I were unwilling to accept my emotions – which in this case amounted to not being comfortable hearing about his ex-girlfriend. Whether I stayed or left I would be stuck in an inner conflict between how I would like to feel (to be unaffected) and how I felt (rejected and vulnerable). It would only be a matter of time before life would present me with another situation that would trigger the same feelings and hence the same conflict.

Bottom-line is: what is, is. The number of times in my life that I've wanted to feel different from how I actually did is a large number. However, I've realized that no matter how much I tell myself that I shouldn't feel insecure or self-centered it has never changed the way I felt.

The only way to deal with problems, which in my opinion are nothing but resistance to "what is" either outside or inside myself (at the end of the day it's two sides of the same coin), is to accept this moment as it is. It also means embracing the emotions I'm not proud of such as anger, jealousy, envy, shame, guilt, arrogance, self-pity etc. Just to sit with these emotions without acting upon them straight away is very powerful.

If it's that simple, why do I find it difficult to do? Because I'm accustomed to believing every thought that goes through my mind. I forget that thoughts are just ideas. What are ideas made of? Nothing. In this perspective it seems obvious that thoughts have little to do with reality. To put it in Mark Twain's words: *"I am an old man and have known a great many troubles, but most of them never happened."*

No matter what, life will always give me something to deal with. If nothing else I've got my flow of uncontrollable thoughts. I've noticed that even when I get what I want the satisfaction doesn't last long. A new "issue" is waiting to be dealt with. This can only lead me to conclude that getting what I want in life is not the recipe for a life filled with joy, gratefulness and inner peace. To me the only option left is to want what I have because that's what I got. Why fight it?

Once I realize that what I have is what I want, the conflict and tension disappear. A problem or unpleasant challenge (which usually manifests itself as a thought or emotion) becomes a gentle reminder to me that I'm fighting "what is", reality as it is this moment. It shows me that I need to stop resisting and start embracing it.

This shift in perception doesn't mean that I shouldn't take action and that I can't ask for what I want. On the contrary. It means that I'm free to act and directly ask for what I want without manipulation and control. If I don't get what I want, it's because I don't need it in that situation. I can ask someone else or do without. When I want what I have I'm open to *all* possibilities and much freer to take appropriate action.

To paraphrase Byron Katie: why wait to be happy until I've achieved my goals – be it getting a university degree, a bigger house, a new boyfriend, a slimmer body? Why not skip the middleman and be happy from here? That's the only place – here and now – where I can experience happiness anyway. The magical side effect of this willingness to embrace life as it is in this moment, is that it not only gives me the space to live in harmony with the way things are (isn't that what love is anyway?) but it also allows me to be that space for others.

Day 264 – September 5, 2007. Cartagena, Colombia

First, I have to write about something that happened yesterday. Just before six o'clock, I got pulled over by a large "Retén Militar" (a police road block) a couple of miles before San Jacinto and two hours south of Cartagena. A police officer dressed in camouflage noticed that they had just pulled over a woman on a motorcycle and let out a big "WOW".

A man in civilian with the best eyes I'd seen in a long, long time came up to me and asked to see my papers. His eyes made me melt completely. He was very handsome too. Less than five minutes earlier I had stopped to put on my rain pants and a couple of lovely plastic bags over my trekking boots. Dark clouds were threatening with rain and for a change I wanted to be prepared. However, in the presence of this handsome man I felt rather awkward in my formless junkyard-version of a rain suit.

I asked the man if it was dangerous to ride in the dark and he replied that it was safe. The police were there to make it safe on the roads and I had nothing to worry about. I asked if they had had a lot of rain and he replied that it hadn't rained while implying that the rain was nothing to be concerned about either. Somehow he did everything he could to reassure me that I had nothing to worry about.

He looked through my papers and told me that everything was okay and that I could continue – then adding with a smile: "Will you take me with you?" I felt like saying yes but instead I turned around and looked at my backpack I had tied to the back of my seat and said: "No hay lugar – lo siento" (I don't have room – sorry). I put Dakar in gear and continued.

As I rode on I felt happy and unconcerned and this feeling grew within me. It was wonderful. Shortly after I had left the "Retén Militar" the rain started pouring down and the darkness of the evening filled the sky. I knew I was safe even though I was riding alone through "guerilla land". Perhaps I didn't need to worry so much about all kinds of things? I felt the goodness and importance of the ability to instill faith and absence of worry in others. When I met the man with the wonderful eyes I guess I needed to feel safe – just for a brief moment.

Maintenance and system relief
Be still

The supreme truth is the most difficult for us to swallow. You are complete and whole as you are. There is nothing to be attained.

Genpo Roshi

It was three in the afternoon. I had an hour to departure. I was in southern Patagonia in Chile waiting for the ferry in Chaitén to bring me to Castro on the island of Chiloé. At four o'clock there was still no sign of the ferry. Two hours later the ferry arrived. It looked like a chunk of floating junk and I had just spent three hours on a boulder by the dock waiting for it.

I parked my motorcycle on the deck and went inside to find my seat. I had been assigned Seat 31. Over the last row of chairs a green sign informed me that the two seats to the right of the aisle were Seat 31 and 30. The distance between the rows suggested they had been designed for dwarves.

The crossing took eight hours. During most of the crossing, to my delight, Seat 30 remained empty. At one point a young Chilean guy sat next to me, presuming that we were going to get to know each other. He quickly realized that this wasn't going to happen.

I got Thoreau's Walden out and tried to read without luck. I hadn't slept well for weeks and I found it difficult to concentrate.

Shortly after a Chilean boy with Downs Syndrome sat down on Seat 30. The first thing the boy did was stare uninhibitedly at me. I looked back smiling at the boy and his companion, a young and handsome man. Ugh. The young man told the boy not to stare at me to which the boy nodded. Then he placed his jacket in the boy's lap to keep him warm and left.

Immediately after the young man had left, the boy resumed his staring at me. It made it difficult to continue my reading of Walden. I looked back at the boy. Our eyes briefly met. Then he turned his head and stared straight ahead with the most wonderful expression I had ever seen. His small eyes were fixated on something right before him even though I was sure he wasn't seeing anything. He used all his energy to pretend he hadn't looked at me. In fact, it was something he wouldn't dream of. Here, innocence itself in its purest and most virginal form was sitting. I *had* to be aware of that. For a while he kept this expression until he collapsed in a knowing giggle. I was completely sold.

This séance repeated itself numerous times while the boy kept himself occupied with other doings. First, he emptied a bag of chips and a Sprite. The empty bag became the object of intense study. It would have been a harmless thing to do if it hadn't been for a foul smell from the bag. I presumed cheese flavor had been added to the contents.

The young handsome man returned to check up on the boy and took away the greasy bag. Unlike the boy, the young man paid no attention to me. What a shame.

I was relieved to be rid of the foul cheese smell but that was only because I didn't know what was coming next. With the bag gone, what was the boy now supposed to do with his hands? I can't say if it was for want of something better to do or if it was caused by the male sex's natural inclinations but what I observed from Seat 31 looked like an intense itch in the boy's crotch, which he energetically treated with his right hand under the jacket. At this point I gave up reading Walden and went out onto the deck to breathe in fresh air.

When I returned to my seat the itch was gone and it remained uneventful on Seat 30 during the rest of the crossing. I was tired and tried to go to sleep but without any luck. I made another attempt with Walden but it was pointless.

At two o'clock in the morning we arrived in Castro. My eyes could scarcely see. I had to find a hostel urgently but that turned out to be easier said than done. Along with a group of cars from the ferry we roamed the desolate streets of Castro to find a vacant room. I had no map of Castro and with a reduced vision I wasn't sure I would be able to find the campsite outside town. I had enough trouble keeping myself and my bike in an upright position.

I stopped outside the office of a taxi company. Two women sat chain smoking in a small barren room. It was the only lighted room on the long quiet street. I went in and asked the women if they could help me find a hostel with a vacant bed. The husband of one of the women entered and the couple offered to take me to a hostel. All I had to do was follow their car. I had no idea where they were taking me. It was pitch black but I wasn't worried. If there was a chance of me laying my tired body in a bed I was willing to do whatever it took – well, almost...

Five minutes later we arrived at a hostel. The couple quickly woke up the owner. Through the intercom the owner said that the hostel was "completo" but when he came to the door and saw the lonely woman with her motorcycle the hostel seemed to be less "completo". His wife appeared in the door too and when she also caught sight of me they suddenly had a vacant bed if I didn't mind sharing a room with a girl from New Zealand. I immediately accepted the offer. I would happily have slept on my inflatable mattress on the floor. They even had a bed for Dakar – a fine parking space behind a locked gate.

I still remember the moments next to the Chilean boy and roaming the empty streets of Castro as if it were yesterday. These moments had an aliveness I didn't experience often on my journey. Such moments only came about when my mind went quiet, when I was still inside. It had nothing to do with what was actually happening in the moment. Because my mind wasn't consumed entirely by thinking I was able to experience the "isness", the completeness of each moment. Perhaps it's more accurate to say that in these moments I became aware of the backdrop against which each experience is experienced.

Not only during most of my motorcycle journey, but for most of my life I have been consumed by thinking, believing myself to be whatever my thoughts told me. I used to believe that I could find every answer through thinking.

I had gone to South America to find out what I wanted to do with my life and I hadn't come up with any answers. Instead I had been confronted with the same type of conflicts and problems as before I left. I was still seeing the world my way and hence creating the same situations. Only the surroundings and the people had changed.

At one point after finishing my trip and returning to Denmark I had the thought: Now, I have to come up with another plan that can outdo my solo motorcycle journey through the Americas. I can't go back to normal life. I have to challenge myself and that means that the next challenge needs to be bigger than the previous one.

I considered doing another ride – this time on the Silk Road with a couple of women who were also into long distance motorcycle traveling. But whenever I thought about being back on the bike on rough dirt roads the exhaustion and unhappiness I had experienced on my ride through Latin America became acutely present in my mind. I felt certain that I would end up getting myself killed if I ventured on another ride of the dimension I had just undertaken.

Then what? At this point two and a half years had passed since I quit my law job and I still didn't know what to do with my life. I looked at my to-do-list. I had to call my dentist to make an appointment, mount lights on my bicycle, buy a birthday present. On it went. It couldn't get more trivial. I took another look at the list and thought to myself: this is the content of my life right now. What am I going to do about it? Escape or deal with it?

I knew only too well that if I tried to escape I would find myself with a similar list. It might sound more exotic to "change oil", "clean and lube chain", "find new tires" but at the end of the day it was just another to-do-list, which would get as tedious as the one I was looking at now. If I kept on treating everything I did as a means to an end I would end up not having lived at all. I would still be waiting for the next big thing, person or event to save me. It would be a continuation of the life I wanted to leave behind. I knew I couldn't go back to living like that.

During my journey I had often made myself miserable in order to get somewhere. When I felt the first pangs of hunger while riding I wouldn't stop to eat. I would continue riding for hours before, at the end of the day, when I had reached my planned destination, I felt I had "time" to eat. At this point my body would be so exhausted that once I started eating I couldn't stop. I usually ended up eating so much that I got a stomachache and then I would torture myself with thoughts about why I couldn't stop eating when full.

When I began to feel cold I wouldn't immediately stop and put on warmer clothes. I would keep on riding until the cold made me virtually numb. Or if I had to go to the restroom I would keep on riding until my bladder seemed at risk of exploding. Even when I was exhausted I forced myself to continue. I had to keep on moving until I arrived at my planned destination. Only then, my thoughts told me, would I be able to feel safe and allow myself to be comfortable.

When I finally allowed myself some rest I was usually unable to do so. The physical exhaustion turned me into a zombie. Sometimes I would stay for a week in a place without doing anything. I didn't see any sights or try to engage in conversations with the people I met. I was laying about, usually in my tent or in a hostel bed, either reading, listening to music or trying to sleep without luck. I didn't get many nights of good sleep.

Even though I was under no time pressure, on the entire journey I felt pressed for time when I was on the bike. I never felt I could truly relax until I reached the day's destination. Without exception, just before arriving I felt a soothing stillness and a sense of being safe that allowed me to loosen up.

When the stillness surfaced, I *knew* it had been present from the beginning of the ride – not present in every experience but as every experience. I just hadn't paid attention to it. I often wondered how I could have missed it. How could I ride an entire day worrying about the condition of the dirt road, the weather or whatever the mind's agenda happened to be and not notice this calming and joyful stillness?

Don't get me wrong. My worries when riding in desolate areas about having a crash, being injured and no one finding me were real concerns. It could happen. I didn't carry a personal tracking device. I was alone and no one knew where I was. However, that I was unsafe wasn't reality. It was a mind game. Reality, when these thoughts went through my head, was that I was on my bike and I was okay.

Just before arriving at my destination the mind game naturally came to a stop. The evidence that I was safe and okay had become too overwhelming. I was so close to my goal that even to my mind it seemed implausible that I was unsafe.

This innocent overlooking rests on the fact that my mind mistakenly links the unveiling of stillness and joy with the attainment of my goal. My mind thinks that reaching my goal is the proof of having made it. Not until I've made it, can I know that I'm okay and safe. Only then I can relax. The reasoning is logical, but it is deluded.

My mind is always trying to interpret what's going on. It's a magnificent tool and it's very useful. But it's just a tool. It can never know the peace that is always present.

Whenever the stillness and sense of being safe surfaced my mind's response was: "yes, I'm okay right now *but...*" If I go down that road there won't be an end to reasons why I can't feel okay right now. However, this moment is all I've ever got. I can't be okay in five minutes. In five minutes I'll experience the moment as "this" moment.

When I don't inquire into the truth of the beliefs that run through my mind, the stillness and joy that is always present will keep evading me no matter what I achieve in life. Yes, of course I will experience some degree of satisfaction when I've reached my goal. But it doesn't last.

It's my experience that this stillness and joy is never caused by any attainment. They are unveiled – regardless of what is happening – when all effort to reach something other than "what is" comes to an absolute end. When I surrender to this moment *as it is* – not my story about it – the simplicity of it offers tremendous relief and clarity on how to proceed.

THE BEGINNING

INNOCENCE AND OPENNESS

Day 256 – August 28, 2007, Medellin, Colombia

The following morning, I rode with Camilo, a Colombian rider I had met in Peru with his girlfriend, to Rionegro where Camilo's family and his girlfriend Vicky live. It was an unbelievable hot day but the ride was amazing. I really enjoyed riding with Camilo. He's a good rider and I enjoyed having him take the lead. I didn't have to think about what roads to take, all I had to do was follow him.

I have to admit that sometimes I feel exhausted riding alone, having to deal with everything myself. Sometimes it's wonderful to have someone by your side. I had this thought when I watched Vicky jump on the back of Camilo's bike in Rionegro. Just once in a while I wouldn't mind jumping on the back of a bike and leave the riding to someone else.

On our way to Rionegro, Camilo and I passed the ruins of Pablo Escobar's Hacienda Napoles. Over the entrance of the hacienda, Escobar had placed a small airplane, which according to Camilo was the first airplane he had used for smuggling cocaine into the United States. The hacienda itself was enormous. Escobar had several houses on the grounds, swimming pools, artificial lakes, a collection of old automobiles (now burnt out) and a zoo. Apparently, there were still sixteen hippos and a couple of zebras around. However, two hippos had escaped and now live in the nearby

Río Magdalena. I guess I won't go swimming there...

No doubt this place had been astounding when Escobar was living here. It was surreal to ride my bike on this piece of land. The area now belongs to the Colombian government and they're planning to build a prison and a zoo. Weird combo if you ask me.

After our visit to Hacienda Napoles we took a rest and a swim in the beautiful Río Claro. A river so crystal-clear, it's hard to believe. As we made our way along the river we passed an outpost with a gorgeous view over the river below. As the most natural thing Camilo suggested that we jumped into the river from the outpost. I looked down and estimated the jump to be about 17 feet. Consequently I was mostly concerned about the river being deep enough. Camilo assured me that it was safe to jump.

I put my sarong and camera down and without hesitation walked to the edge and jumped. In mid air I realized that the jump was closer to twice the distance I had thought. Fuck, I was scared! It was a weird sensation being in mid air just waiting to hit the water. When touch down finally took place I was so tensed up by fear in my neck and jaw that it was a very painful plunge. I actually felt pain in my teeth and jaw the rest of the day.

It's funny because when I jumped I made a silly scream, which during my descent turned into a gargling sound of deep fear. After my jump a rather surprised Camilo followed suit.

Once in the river he told me that he was sure that I wasn't going to jump. Well, if he had told me that the jump was thirty-five feet there was no way I would have freaking done it! I don't know, I think I'm getting too old for games like this. I honestly can't be bothered to run around doing crazy shit to prove my courage.

Accidents and first aid
Yield

Nothing to win, nothing to lose.

Lao Tzu

On my first day of riding in Panama I got a taste of what the riding experience in Central America was going to be like. Rain every single day. Most places it wasn't even warm. Riding with deficient rain gear didn't help since it more often than not left me soaked after being caught in the rain. I had decided against buying new rain gear thinking at this point I might as well finish the trip without. Why leave the job undone?

I was beginning to wish that the whole trip would come to an end. While in Colombia I had finally bought my plane ticket home from Los Angeles and I was now able to see the end to the journey. I was exhausted from traveling alone for eleven months. I dreamt about being at home in Denmark in my own bed, not having to seek out a new place to stay every night, spending hours on the bike each day.

Now, I had made it to Central America and I was so close to my goal of reaching Los Angeles that, no matter what, I wasn't going to give up. I mobilized every bit of remaining energy I had left in my tired body and got through hours of riding in the rain. By the time I made it to Mexico City all I had left was an easy week's ride. The weather had even dried up. I was finally within reach of my goal and I was vividly imaging what it would feel like riding into Los Angeles after a year on the road.

I spent five days in Mexico City. I still wasn't sleeping much and mentally I felt like I had been sucked into a black hole and turned into black matter. It was no fun being in my own company. I desperately needed sleep and to regain strength. However, I never considered staying longer to recuperate in Mexico City.

You see, I had a plan and with the bulldozer approach still being in operation I was going to stick with that plan. My American relatives in Los Angeles had invited me to join them for Thanksgiving, which was a week away. I was determined to get there in time for the celebration. This gave me a week in Los Angeles before my anticipated yet terrifying return to Denmark became reality. It was the perfect plan.

On the day of my planned departure from Mexico City I hadn't slept at all and the first strong feeling that hit me as I got up in the morning was: "I can't ride today. It's impossible". Then I started crying.

Slowly, I began to pack and make plans for the day. I decided to leave Mexico City and find a quiet hotel in the countryside where I could get a good night's sleep. The worst traffic would then be behind me and the following day I would be ready for a long ride farther north.

I didn't have a road map of Mexico City so when I got to the first highway entrance I was unsure where to go. I waved down a Mexican rider and asked if he was heading north out of town. I was in luck. He was on his way north too and offered to guide me out of the enormous city. All I had to do was follow him.

We rode onto the highway and I felt immensely relieved. My worries about getting out of Mexico City without a map or GPS suddenly seemed silly. Now, I had my own guide who would lead me safely out of one of the Americas' biggest cities with twenty million inhabitants. It couldn't get any easier.

At the exact time these thoughts went through my head a red car in the middle lane made a quick turn to catch an exit on the right, thereby trying to cross the right lane where I happened to be. The left side of my handlebar received a blow and for what felt like an eternity I struggled to keep the rubber side of my tires down. I didn't make it.

In the fall I blacked out and the next thing I was aware of was the most excruciating pain I had experienced in my life. A moment later the pain was gone and I felt I was outside my body, somewhere above to the left. In that moment, the pain was so intense that I couldn't feel it. It seemed like everything became one, as if I had ceased to exist – or at least my body and my personality had ceased to exist. It was the most extraordinary sensation I had ever experienced.

The pain regained its force and I was unmistakably back in my own skin. I must have been screaming like an animal because the people who had gathered around me didn't dare come near me. From a safe distance they shouted to me that I shouldn't move.

The first thing I did when I heard this was move. The pain came from my left leg and I had to feel if it was still there. It was there all right. I had slid along the highway till my left knee hit the curb and made my body and bike come to a halt. My left knee had been squashed between the curb and my bike.

I was in shock. I couldn't believe that this was happening. One week before I was supposed to reach my goal a car had hit me. I was living my worst nightmare. No, it was beyond my worst nightmare. Not even in my wildest worst-case scenarios had I been able to come up with this. The universe had scored a big point against me. My goalkeeper must have been on a picnic because in a million years I hadn't seen this coming.

Yet as I lay by the curb I had a clear feeling of being okay. I had no reason and no data to rely on that could support this feeling but it was nonetheless there. Even though my mind was filled with scary thoughts about my future, a deeper and inexplicable knowing told me that I was okay.

Slowly, my crying subsided enough for people around to dare come near me. The rider who had offered to be my guide called an ambulance and the driver of the red car came up to me and took upon himself full responsibility, a rare and almost bizarre occurrence in Latin America where many drivers don't have insurance and are therefore nowhere to be seen if they're involved in an accident and can get away.

The ambulance arrived and the paramedics asked me what hospital I wanted to go to. I had no idea and asked for a recommendation. They told me they weren't allowed to give advice on the choice of hospital. Luckily, a Mexican Harley rider, who had passed the scene of the accident and had stopped to offer his assistance, came to my rescue. He let me use his cell phone to make a call to the Danish Embassy. I happened to have their phone number in my tank bag. It was the day of the parliamentary election in Denmark and a couple of days earlier I had done my citizen's duty and put in my vote at the embassy.

The embassy told me to go to Hospital Español. Still in shock I was put on a stretcher and carried into the ambulance. The Mexican rider made sure I got all my belongings with me and promised to take care of my motorcycle. If it hadn't been for this man it's very likely that my motorcycle as well as my belongings on the bike would have been stolen.

Once in the ambulance I thought my troubles were over but it turned out they had just begun. Apparently, the driver of the red car had called his insurance company and they had sent a man to the scene of the accident to have a chat with – not their client, but with me. I couldn't believe my own eyes. I was alone and in shock and pain. I was 6,000 miles away from my family and friends, laying in an ambulance on a highway in Mexico City. How could they possibly think I would be in the mood to talk to a representative of an insurance company? Someone had a sick sense of humor.

First, the insurance man tried to persuade me to go to a different hospital, claiming that his company didn't cover my treatment at Hospital Español. This hospital wasn't on their list of approved hospitals. Sobbing I told him I only wanted to go to Hospital Español because I didn't know anything about the hospitals he had suggested. I was going to stick with the recommendation from the Danish Embassy. I had the best travel insurance money could buy. If the insurance company of the driver who had hit me wasn't going to pay, then my insurance company would. And if they wouldn't pay, then I would. I wasn't about to risk my health because of a cheeky insurance man.

My reasoning didn't seem to create much understanding with Mr. Insurance and it wasn't until I started crying hard and being seemingly out of control that he realized that the woman on the stretcher wasn't going to give in.

He left the ambulance and returned a minute later. Mr. Insurance wasn't going to give up that easily either. He was down one point and needed a new approach. This time he handed me a piece of paper and asked me to sign. At first I was speechless. Then crying hard, I explained to him that in my current condition I was incapable of signing anything. I turned my head the other way and let a big amount of tears and snot out of my face.

Finally, he left and as the ambulance began to move, one of the paramedics took my hand and said to me: "It was very wise of you not to sign that paper".

Now, I had arrived at a point beyond consolation. I just kept on crying, not so much because of the pain – my leg kept a surprisingly low profile – but because I was beginning to realize the consequences of the accident. That I wasn't going to reach the goal I had set for myself: a goal that had been just for me, not because it made me fit in or because it would look good on my résumé. It had been my goal because it had felt right to me.

I tried to explain my situation to the paramedics but I doubt my Spanish mixed with tears and snot made any sense to them. One of them kept holding my hand. It was a tiny gesture but in that moment, it meant the world to me. Without it I felt I would have disappeared from the face of the earth.

We arrived at the hospital and I immediately underwent several examinations. I had been exceedingly lucky. The doctors examined me with disbelief. I hadn't broken anything. The impact with the curb followed by a squeeze from Señor Dakar had only left me with a sizeable hematoma in my left leg and an all round beaten up body.

I was taken to a private room in the ER where three young doctors were present while a fourth one put my left leg in a bandage. An employee from the hospital administration came by and asked for my insurance papers. Earlier, a diplomat from the Danish Embassy had been to see me and I had borrowed his cell phone and called my insurance company in Denmark. They told me they would cover all the bills and that I didn't have to worry about anything.

I handed the admin person my insurance card along with the number of the company's twenty-four hour telephone service and sighed with relief. It was nine o'clock in the evening, nine hours had passed since the accident and I suddenly noticed that I was hungry and very thirsty.

The hematoma in my leg, which had monopolized half a gallon of my blood, combined with the overall excitement of the day, months of lack of sleep plus the general exhaustion from almost a year on the road alone, were beginning to kick in. I felt beyond weak.

I asked to go to the bathroom. A nurse brought me a bedpan but I insisted on having enough strength to go to the bathroom myself. I didn't. As it turned out I was unable to walk. I was put in a wheelchair and taken to the bathroom. Getting my body from the wheelchair to the toilet seat almost made me faint. As I was taken back to my bed I felt I had run a marathon. A doctor put an IV in my right arm, which was attached to a tube of bright yellow fluid. It looked like pee. My hunger seemed to be going away but I was still incredible thirsty.

Upon my request a nurse produced the smallest cup of water I had ever seen. I slurped it down in a split second. I guess I was then supposed to be ready for the next set of problems.

The admin woman reappeared and told me that they couldn't get hold of my insurance company and that I had to pay upfront. I was surprised to hear this since the number I had given them was a twenty-four hour hotline. However, at this point I had no energy to battle with anyone so I handed the woman my credit card and expected the problem to go away.

Ten minutes later she returned and informed me that my credit card had been rejected. I realized that the amount they had tried to withdraw from my account exceeded the limit of my allowed monthly withdrawal. I told the admin woman that I would call my bank the following day. Because of the time difference my bank was closed and I had no way of raising the limit that evening. Upon hearing this, the admin person told me that I had to leave the hospital.

Was there going to be no end to bad news this day? I was back to being in shock. I couldn't walk and I didn't have any friends or family I could stay with in Mexico City who would be able to look after me. Before the accident I had stayed with a Danish friend but he had gone to Monterey in northern Mexico on business for a week. If I ended up in the wrong taxi late at night in Mexico City (and considering the increasingly bad luck I had attracted during the day the chances seemed relatively high) I would be out of business for good.

While pondering upon the latest developments and shedding more tears a female doctor I hadn't seen before walked in and informed me that a nurse would shortly arrive to remove the IV. It was eleven o'clock at night and the hospital staff seemed to think I was now ready for a night in town, pouring down cocktails while making wild disco moves on a dance floor. I had a different perspective on my night in town and it didn't seem very appealing.

Half an hour later the female doctor returned and asked if the nurse had removed the IV. At this point my final meltdown took place. I realized that they were actually going to let me leave the hospital in the condition I was in. Over my dead body was I going to let them help me with such a thing. I wanted nothing to do with people like them. From now on I was going to take action myself.

I started crying hard and screamed that if they didn't remove the IV straight away I would pull it out of my arm myself. At the same time I tried to get out of the hospital bed on the opposite side of the IV's attachment to the tube. I wanted to get as far away as possible from the hospital. If they thought it was okay to treat their patients this way, they were wrong! I was furious.

The amount of noise and commotion I created made several doctors and nurses come to the door and I guess they finally realized that I wasn't capable of taking care of myself. A couple of minutes later the admin woman returned with a piece of paper and told me to sign. If I signed they would admit me to the hospital. Crying I signed the paper realizing that I had no idea what I was signing. All I knew was that I didn't have the strength to leave.

At one o'clock in the morning I finally got something to eat and drink and in that moment it felt like the best meal I had eaten in my life. I seriously doubt it was the case. I pushed away the tray and I fell asleep.

During the following week the admin woman returned dutifully to my room each day and asked for money. She said that if my insurance company didn't pay I would have to leave the hospital. The thought of having to leave felt so daunting that she might as well have pointed a gun at me. I wasn't able to cope with even the slightest change.

I kept calling and emailing my insurance company and they continually told me that they were taking care of everything and that one of their Spanish-speaking agents in Miami was on the case. They didn't understand why the hospital kept hassling me for money.

On my seventh day in the hospital the admin woman's daily visit happened while I was on the phone to my insurance company's agent. He asked to speak with the woman and I handed over the phone.

I have no idea what he said but from my bed I could observe that her face went pale. The only words that came out of her mouth were the occasional "si, si" and then she hung up. That was the last I saw of her. I can't say I missed her even though I wasn't overburdened with visitors while in hospital.

The first three days I spent crying. I made sure the hospital staff didn't catch me in my crying sessions. I put on a happy face when they were around. I don't know why. I didn't feel like talking to them about what had happened. My insurance company asked me if I needed to talk to a trauma therapist. I didn't even consider it. Of course I didn't need to speak to a therapist. My refusal to speak to a therapist had nothing to do with pride. I was convinced I didn't need one.

I felt strangely relieved to be in the hospital. At times I even felt happy. Now, I had a legitimate excuse to let other people take care of me. I didn't have to do anything. If I needed help I could ring a bell. Meals appeared by themselves and my bed was made for me. Every decision was out of my hands and it was just what I needed. I loved it.

The only stress I experienced, besides dealing with the admin woman's quest for money, was my own unwillingness to give up the idea of continuing my journey. I still wanted to reach my goal and finish my trip in Los Angeles. However, I couldn't walk and after I'd had a rare shower, I felt I was able to sleep for a million years. Yet it didn't prevent me from making plans to get my bike fixed and ride to Los Angeles.

After three days of crying and trying to figure out a clever plan to continue I finally gave up. I accepted that under no circumstances was I fit to travel by motorcycle. Whether I liked it or not my journey had ended in Mexico City, one week before I was supposed to reach my goal. I surrendered.

In that moment a profound shift occurred. I noticed that nothing had changed since the accident. Absolutely *nothing* had changed. I was the same as I was three days ago, before the accident. It blew my mind. My *immediate* experience of who I am was exactly the same in the hospital as it was three days earlier when I was riding my motorcycle. Experientially I realized that my failure to reach my goal of riding to Los Angeles didn't affect me in any way.

I guess the best way to describe this realization is that I clearly experienced who I am – or maybe it's more accurate to say "that I am" – beyond thinking. Without any thought about who or what I am, what's left? I can't put words to it but what I did realize through direct, immediate experience was that whatever I am, it can't be affected by anything that happens. No matter how "wrong" things seem to go – or how well for that matter – on a deeper level it can never affect "that I am".

Four hundred years ago Shakespeare let Hamlet put it like this: *"For there is nothing either good or bad, but thinking makes it so"*. I guess some news don't travel *that* fast.

Day 355 – December 6, 2007, Mexico City, Mexico

I don't understand what's happening. I'm trying to find a way to get Dakar out of Mexico and it seems impossible. At the same time I don't feel like shipping Dakar home. I would like to come back to Mexico and ride to Los Angeles – or is that what I really want? As I wrote these words I didn't feel like returning to Mexico and finishing the ride.

Yesterday, I felt that leaving Dakar behind was some kind of insurance policy. If I don't like being at home in Denmark I can get back on the bike and continue traveling. Is that really why I don't feel like shipping Dakar home? Sometimes I feel I have to return to finish the trip. I can't explain why. But is it right? Am I trying to make another escape from myself or am I listening to my inner voice?

It looks like I won't be able to find a container for Dakar but I'm afraid of making the final decision to let him stay in Mexico City. I felt exactly the same way when I had to book my ticket to go to Buenos Aires. When Mariano offered me the job at Motocare I felt deep joy and knew I just had to go. Time passed and when I had to book my plane ticket, I kept postponing it because fear of making the wrong decision had crept in.

This morning I thought about my injured knee and I realized that it was the first time I had paid attention to "my little elephant" since the accident. It was the first time I thought about how my knee could get well. All my thoughts have concerned Dakar and his shipment. I can't continue like this. I have to learn to take care of myself and that's what I'm learning now.

.....

Now, I've told the mechanic that Dakar is staying in Mexico City and that I would like to get him repaired. The decision has been made. It feels great. I went to see Dakar today and I was happy to see him. I miss him.

Earlier today I collapsed at the physiotherapy at the hospital. I've run myself down completely. It's such a relief that I've made the decision to let Dakar stay. Now I can concentrate on my knee and start taking care of myself. I feel very frustrated. I feel that no one at home understands me. I'm frustrated because they don't seem to care. All I've heard is: "You'll manage". As I wrote these words I felt like crying.

I've just realized that I haven't wanted to touch my knee. A physiotherapist in Denmark I've been in contact with, told me to massage my knee. My physiotherapist here in Mexico City massages it with some kind of apparatus but I haven't touched the knee myself. I've actually felt revolted by it and I haven't been willing to acknowledge its existence. The knee had to heal quickly on its own. Just like that. It upsets me that I've neglected my knee, my health and myself. It makes me very upset.

I've been afraid to touch the knee. I felt disgusted by it even though in some way I've appreciated it and thought it was cute. But the knee wasn't something I was willing to deal with. It had to cope on its own. No sweet Mommy here.

Why have I been afraid to touch the knee? I thought it was revolting, that it wasn't a part of me. It didn't belong to me. It was ugly and weak. Fat and disgusting. I didn't want to be associated with it. I'm better than it, stronger than it. Do I not want to acknowledge the part of me that's fat, weak, ugly and helpless? No, I do not. Helpless – that's the word I don't like. To be helpless is to be pathetic – to be worthless. Now I have a knee that's helpless, weak, fat, ugly and which desperately needs help. What do I do? I turn my back on my knee. I couldn't be bothered to take care of it. And this way I've turned my back on myself. Tears are welling up inside me.

Yesterday, I was upset because I felt my parents didn't understand me. I desperately wanted them to understand me. But the thing is, I haven't given them the chance. I've pretended to be okay and on top of things even though I wasn't. Now that I need them I push them away.

Crossing the finish line
Share

*We spend a whole life searching for a miracle
and what we fail to realize is
that life is the miracle.
All of it.*

Anonymous

I spent four months in Denmark after the accident in Mexico City. The first two weeks I spent in my apartment, I was reluctant to settle in. It took me a while to pick up my boxes at my brother's place and once I got them I didn't unpack.

I sat in the empty apartment and felt estranged. I felt everything was the same as when I had left twenty-one months earlier and yet I felt everything was different. I didn't want to see anyone. I cried for no apparent reason. I could be walking in the streets and suddenly feel the tears pressing. I would rush home and cry. When I went to the grocery store I felt sick being surrounded by food. I left the store without buying anything. At times I felt numb and disconnected. At times I felt ecstatic. I had no idea how to navigate in my home environment. Everything was familiar to me and yet I didn't know how to act.

Slowly, things began to change. I took one step at a time and refrained from worrying about the future. I was aware of the fact that my energy was limited and that I would do best to avoid overloading myself with new activities and projects. I allowed myself to recover from the accident and to digest my experiences. Instinctively, I knew it was a process I couldn't rush. At the time the emotions and thoughts that surfaced didn't make sense to me. I didn't try to avoid them. Whichever of them wanted to surface, I let surface and then I dealt with them from there.

Usually, it was enough for me to become aware of the emotions and thoughts for them to let go of me. I was surprised how quickly my emotions and thoughts changed when I didn't fight them. After a month at home thoughts about returning to Mexico City to finish my journey appeared.

I was acutely aware of the fact that if I returned to Mexico it could be another attempt to escape from myself. This time I was determined not to run. I felt I had become strong enough to deal with whatever was coming my way.

I had no clue about what I wanted to do with my life. While traveling I thought that when I returned to Denmark I would have found my calling. I often felt the internal pressure of coming up with "the grand plan" for life. The more I felt the pressure the more out of reach a plan had become. The further I felt from coming up with a plan the more scared I had been about returning to Denmark.

During the last two months of my journey the anxiety about my future had been building up. As chance would have it the accident took care of this anxiety and forced me to refocus and deal with current matters. In every conceivable way my accident, which at first had seemed like one of the worst things to happen to me, turned out to be one of my biggest blessings.

In regard to my plan for the future there was only one way to describe my Latin American adventure: a total disaster. I went away to figure out my life and two years later I returned with a left knee the size of a basketball and a plan matching that of a goldfish.

I had returned with more unanswered questions than I had before I left. I was overwhelmed and there was only one thing to do. I had to deal with it – whatever "it" happened to be.

I wanted to return to Mexico City and finish my trip but I had several concerns. First of all, I didn't want to run from my problems so if another trip meant that I was running away I didn't want to go. Secondly, I was scared about getting back on the bike. I had been extremely lucky to escape the accident without any permanent damage. In fact, I could easily have been killed. Was I willing to risk my life in order to finish a trip that was just an idea in my head? Perhaps the accident was a sign that I should stop before it was too late. And thirdly, I needed to come up with a plan for earning some money. I hadn't earned any money since I quit my law job. I still had some savings but they weren't going to last forever. I wanted to come up with a new way of making a living before I ran out of funds.

Since the accident I had been in contact with a rider in Pennsylvania in the States who had been a great support to me. I had gotten in contact with him through Horizons Unlimited, a website for long distance motorcycle riders. After the accident in Mexico City I posted a thread on the site and asked for help to get my bike out of Mexico. Chris, the rider in Pennsylvania, responded and we stayed in contact.

In an email I mentioned to him that I wanted to go back to Mexico City but that I had to come up with a plan for earning some money too. He suggested that I share my experiences of my motorcycle journey with other riders. He knew a couple of people who had successfully done so.

Up till that point it hadn't occurred to me that anyone would be interested in hearing about my motorcycle journey and my futile attempt to figure out my life. When push came to shove what did I know about motorcycling? I had launched myself into it and had made most of the mistakes possible.

The idea of sharing my experiences seemed foreign to me and yet it struck a chord within me. I felt uplifted by the fact that I had managed to pull off something I thought I could never do. And if I of all people – not knowing anything about motorcycles, not speaking Spanish and with very limited experience traveling alone in developing countries – could pull it off, then anybody could. It seemed like a good message to share.

I began to see my journey in a different light. Instead of focusing on my failures I began to see what I had learned from them. I didn't stop to think if I was on the right track or not. I just sat down and began to put words to the lessons I had learned and tried to find an angle and a platform for how I might share my experiences with others. Before long I was working on a text for a website to promote myself as a keynote speaker.

I hired a web designer, consulted with friends and three months after I had returned to Denmark I launched a website and a new career as a speaker. I had no idea how I was going to put together my talk and what exactly I would be sharing with people. At the time it wasn't a concern to me. I knew what my core message was and what I stood for. Or maybe it's more accurate to say I knew what I didn't stand for and felt it was more than enough to get started.

Meanwhile, I seriously began to consider going back to Mexico City to finish the trip. I had been one week away from my goal – Los Angeles. I felt I had left something undone. However, it seemed silly to ride the short distance from Mexico City to Los Angeles and then catch a flight home. Instead I came up with the idea of riding across the United States to New York.

My worries about making another escape by returning to Mexico began to seem unreal. However, my fear about getting back on the bike was still undiminished. I had no idea how to overcome it – or even if I ought to.

I chose a practical approach to the issue at hand. I needed to deal with my motorcycle. I had left it with a mechanic in Mexico City who had promised to repair it. I had no idea whether he had done the repair or if indeed my bike was still at his shop. The first time I met the mechanic I immediately trusted him but I also knew that anything was possible in Latin America. Perhaps the bike had disappeared. I was far away and had no way of checking up on things. If my bike wasn't repaired or if it had mysteriously disappeared in Mexico City then the decision about returning to finish the ride was easy: no bike – no ride.

I wrote an email to the mechanic and asked about my bike. I promised myself that if and when I received an answer I would trust my first spontaneous response to whatever the reply happened to be. And I promised myself I would stick to it even if I later started to feel and think differently.

The following day I found a reply in my inbox. I clicked on the email and started reading. My bike had already been repaired. Dakar was waiting for me to return and the mechanic was looking forward to seeing me soon. An instant sensation of joy and bliss filled my body and a moment later it was so intense that I had to get up and jump around laughing in my apartment.

Despite my past ability to ignore the signals from my body this one was impossible to overlook: I had got to get back in the saddle. I bought a plane ticket to Mexico City and a return ticket from New York and a month later I was on my way.

Four months had passed since the accident. As I got in the saddle and positioned myself I felt the comforting familiarity of my bike. I pressed the ignition, listened to the engine and breathed in. I kicked the side stand up, released the clutch, gently twisted the throttle and felt my body balance the bike into a steady movement. Immediately, an uncontrollable undertow of fear arose. Every muscle in my body tensed up. Every turn I made was a battle against the fear of death. I felt I had launched myself into a horror road movie I wasn't going to survive.

During my first month of riding I had a miserable time on the bike. I tried to minimize the time I spent riding, which with some good reason could be considered a counterproductive activity on a motorcycle journey. Occasionally, I would experience a brief sensation of joy but it quickly drowned in my growing fear of sudden death involving a big truck, my motorcycle and me.

By the time I got to San Francisco I was paralyzed by fear and was unable to continue my journey. I stayed a month under the pretence of wanting to explore the Bay Area. It wasn't a total lie but the real motivation for staying was my fear of riding. I seemed unable to kick the fear that I might have another accident and that next time I wouldn't be so lucky.

I decided to sign up for a dirt-riding clinic in Hollister south of San Francisco. I thought I might ease the fear by improving my riding skills even though I hadn't had the accident on dirt.

Things didn't go according to plan. Half way through the track day we were practicing wheelies. Kari, one of the owners of the BMW motorcycle dealership in Mountain View, smoothly demonstrated the drill. I followed his movements intently, trying to absorb as much as possible before it was my turn to twist the throttle and pop the front wheel.

Nothing happened. My front wheel seemed glued to the track. I decided to give the throttle an extra twist and immediately lost control of the bike. I headed straight for the edge of the track, dug the front wheel into the hillside and banged the left knee I injured in Mexico City head-on into the dirt.

A couple of riders rushed to my rescue to check that I was okay. With every fiber of my body I fought the urge to panic. I didn't want the other riders to think I was a sissy. I managed to withhold most of the tears and put a brave smile on my face. My knee was throbbing with pain. If I indulged – even for a split second – in the physical pain and the pictures I was seeing in my head of a crushed knee, the other riders would have had to put me in the recovery position while they waited for the loony bin to pick me up.

I limped off the track and tried not to think about the situation. I had hit my injured knee again. Surely this had to be a sign that I ought to give up motorcycle riding. I was shocked.

A paramedic arrived at the track and gave me some ice. My knee's head-on collision with the dirt meant that it hadn't been twisted, only severely bruised. I put the ice on the knee and quickly the pain subsided.

Instead of reducing my fear of a motorcycle accident, my track day had resulted in increased fear, a big bruise on my injured knee and a sizable repair bill. Dakar's radiator looked like it had been kicked in by Hulk.

However, I couldn't complain about the location of the accident. People who were more than willing to help me out surrounded me. I arranged with Kari to have Dakar repaired at his shop in Mountain View and, as chance would have it, we got talking about my ride through Latin America. I told him that I was starting up as a speaker and asked him if he was interested in hosting my talk at a customer event at his store. He said he would talk to his partners and see if it was possible to set up an event at short notice.

A couple of days later he called and told me we were on for the following Friday. Argh! This was obviously fantastic news but that only gave me a week to come up with a talk. I had no idea how I was going to deliver my message. All I had was a fancy website and a new career title. Adding content hadn't occurred to me up till this point.

I started brainstorming. My stunt on the track clearly illustrated that I wasn't an expert rider and that I wouldn't attract many listeners if I claimed to be an expert on riding techniques unless making your bike look like it had received a kick from Hulk was something worth learning. I wasn't putting my money on that. It made me think of a quote by Hemingway who wrote: "Whatever success I have had has been through writing what I know about". It seemed plausible the same principle applied to what you talk about.

This was bad news. What did I know about motorcycle riding and traveling? It was a fact that I was not the best rider, not the best planner, not the first woman to do a solo ride through Latin America. Where was all my knowledge going to come from? Suddenly it was patently obvious. From all my mistakes.

Instantly my confidence rose. Okay – what next? I obviously couldn't cover all my mistakes in an hour's talk so I had to select the best – whatever that meant. I decided to go for the mistakes, which had made me suffer the most. In my mind I went through my motorcycle journey and came up with ten situations where I had been so miserable that a visit from Sigourney Weaver's "Alien" would have been preferable.

Two days before my grand premiere I had come up with a talk called "Adventure riding in

Latin America – The Top 10 List of How *Not* to Do It". I had no idea whether I was able to pull it off. For the first time in my life I was putting myself out there one hundred percent. The entire talk was built on my own experiences. I wasn't referring to clever books, law statutes or expert authorities. The show was about me – butt naked.

When I arrived at the BMW Motorcycle store in Mountain View I was surprisingly calm. The fact that I wasn't getting paid certainly had something to do with it. After all, how much can you demand of a total amateur who's sharing her experiences for free? I figured that at most the audience had to endure an hour's agony, which hopefully wouldn't be so painful that they wished "Señor Alien" would swing by and take over.

About eighty people showed up and an hour later I wrapped up my presentation and received overwhelming applause. They seemed to like it. I was amazed. All I had done was truthfully tell my own story. After the presentation people came up to me and thanked me for sharing my experiences. This was definitely good news.

However, it didn't change a thing about my fear of having another motorcycle accident. I still felt that my crash at the track was a clear message for me to stop pushing my luck, to go home, grow up and stop this childish and dangerous nonsense about motorcycling.

I knew it would be self-torture if not suicidal to continue riding with the fear I was experiencing. My riding was unsafe because I was unable to relax on the bike.

I called my friend Ernest back home and explained the situation. He always gave me his truthful perspective on things. He listened carefully as I described my present state of mind. My elaborations didn't leave any aspect of my anxiety untouched even though the word "fruit cake" would have summed it up nicely. When I stopped talking he said: "Annette, you've got two options: you can stop riding a motorcycle or you can stop whining."

At first, this perspective seemed a little unkind. I mean, I had had a serious accident. But as I let his words sink in I knew he was right and, what was more surprising, I also knew that there was no way I was giving up riding a motorcycle. It had all been a show. I had created a drama in my head and received quite a bit of attention on that account but if I had to choose between my drama and my motorcycle, I was in no doubt. Señor Dakar won, hands down.

A couple of days later I loaded my bike, twisted the throttle and crossed the Bay Bridge riding east. The anxiety about having another accident I left behind in San Francisco and to this date it hasn't resurfaced. Just imagine if I had had my fear of falling when I was learning how to walk. I would still be crawling today.

Two months after I had left San Francisco I rode into New York City on a beautiful July summer day. Before I disappeared into the Lincoln Tunnel I caught a glimpse of the

Manhattan skyline. The skyscrapers looked small, almost unreal. I re-emerged on the other side of the Hudson River in the shadow of the tall buildings surrounding me. It was unbelievable hot but the heat didn't get to me. I felt could fly.

As I dug my way through the Manhattan traffic I tried to absorb the fact that I had finally reached my goal. But it was no use. It was too much to comprehend. I felt I was losing the density of my physical body and that I was about to merge with everything that surrounded me.

The midday traffic was heavy and before long I was stuck. Just before reaching Union Square, a guy in a SUV asked me where my number plate was from. A simple question I could answer with one word: Argentina. Instead I chose to fill him in on most of my life story before the traffic started moving again. It was impossible for me to contain the joy I felt inside my body. I *had* to share it. The time I had spent alone on my bike had taught me that when I share the abundance I feel inside, it grows and when I keep it to myself, it shrinks. On this day in New York there was no other option available to me than to share my bliss and let it expand into the universe.

If I were to pick the most important lesson of my motorcycle journey it would be that joy is causeless and for it to expand it needs space, it needs to be shared. I used to believe that joy could only be found outside myself, by achieving something or by adding something to myself. I believed that I was incomplete. I'm not. No one is. Only thinking can make one forget.

However, for joy to be experienced I also have to be willing to embrace its counterpart: sorrow – in whatever form it takes in life. Duality is the game of the universe and I can't have one without the other. If I'm unwilling to accept sorrow, I also shut out joy.

Most of my life my actions have unconsciously been an attempt to either cling to feelings of happiness or escape whatever shape the sorrow or pain inside me has taken, be it rejection, feelings of unworthiness, incompleteness etc. None of my many efforts have worked – at least not for very long.

The reason I found it difficult to stop running is that to meet the sorrow I have to be alone. Not lonely, separated or isolated from others. I can ask for and receive support from my surroundings – that's a sane mind acting, to get help when needed – but I need to walk the last mile alone. Only *I* can directly meet, experience and bear *my* difficult and painful thoughts, feelings, emotions and my physical pain. No one can do it for me and I can't do it for others. But the magic at work is that once I'm willing to be alone – to meet the sorrow fully and directly – the ever-present, impersonal, causeless peace and joy is unveiled.

My journey through the Americas opened my heart and mind to the fact that what I had been looking for and not found – this ever-present joy – I already have. Now, I understand why my anxiety about coming up with a plan for my future grew during the first leg of my journey the closer I got to finishing it. I was looking in all the wrong places. Ironically, it wasn't until three days before my accident in Mexico City that I received the first clear hint about where to look.

I had attended a concert in Mexico City by the world-renowned Danish flautist, Michala Petri and classical guitarist Lars Hannibal. I was familiar with Michala Petri and her story but I had never heard her perform live.

I enjoyed the concert immensely and was deeply moved by her performance. It was executed with utmost sensitivity, great storytelling and playfulness. I was in awe but at the same time I felt sad. I knew that she began playing the recorder when she was three years old and now she was in her late forties. She'd had more than forty years to get *that* good and it was no secret that she had worked hard and practiced for hours each day to get to where she was today. I wondered if I would ever be able to become good at something, having left my legal career at the age of thirty-one after having spent thirteen years of my life in the law. I felt that if I didn't return to practicing law I would have to start from scratch. Ground zero. And where could that possibly take me at the age of thirty-two with an estimated fifty or sixty years to go?

Since I quit my law job I had aimlessly launched myself into a variety of activities: I had learned to ride a motorcycle, how to repair and maintain a motorcycle, I had learned

Spanish and traveled by motorcycle through Latin America. I had undertaken these activities without any greater plan or gain in mind. Those were just things I really wanted to do. But after a year on the road, still without a clue about what to do with my life when my journey came to an end, I found it little uplifting to be in the presence of someone who had dedicated her life to mastering *one* instrument.

When I spoke to Michala after the concert I told her what a joy it had been to listen to her playing but I also confessed that her performance had left me disillusioned when I related it to my own future.

"Will I ever be able to become good at anything?" I asked her without expecting more than a "sure you will."

Instead she answered: "Nobody wants to listen to me play because I have a great technique but because I have something to say, because I have a story to tell. And that's the same with you. You do have a story to tell, all you've got to do is find your instrument."

As she said those words I knew without a shred of doubt that she was right. My story is of those things closest to my heart. I don't have to be the best. All I have to do is be true to myself. Earlier it had never dawned on me to question the belief that I had to be the best at something in order to live a life full of joy and gratitude.

At some point in my life I equated being good at something with being happy, successful and safe. However, being good at something only makes sense if I compare myself to others. Do I feel happy when I compare myself to others and feel better than them? No. On the contrary. In the most joyful moments of my life I lose awareness of myself as a person. In these moments, the story *about* me is absent and I'm at one with whatever I'm doing. The joy that's always here is given room to expand. I have gotten myself out of the way and this allows a story worth telling to be told *through* me.

Day 115 – April 8, 2007. Venado Tuerto, Argentina

After three days in bed with a fever I'm back on the bike. As I get on the bike I don't feel a hundred percent but during the day I begin to feel better. Today, my head is empty and I feel peaceful inside.

When I twist the throttle I feel I'm about to take off – that I'm able to fly. It's difficult to explain why this tiny movement with my right wrist feels so amazing. At the end of the wrist the hand is attached. It's the opening to another world where I can feel my surroundings in a unique way. My hands can sense what they touch and send unfiltered signals back to my brain. It's the same process that's activated when I twist the throttle.

When I twist the throttle, however slightly, a new world opens up and I'm allowed to experience the world in a different way. By twisting the throttle I give life to the machine between my legs. The movements of the machine exposes me to new impressions every millisecond. Time stands still. An explosion of sense perceptions saturates my mind. The mind is silent. It's freedom.

AFTERWORD

When there is no desire,
all things are at peace.

Lao Tzu

"What now? Does she live effortlessly?" you might ask yourself.

I could answer this question with both a yes and a no but if you sincerely want to understand what effortlessness is, it's not the right question to ask.

While traveling I met many people who told me they wanted to do what I was doing — mostly motivated by a wish to escape the commonplace quiet desperation of ordinary life.

In the beginning of my journey I gave people the answer they wanted to hear (which happened to be the answer I wanted to hear too): that it's possible to escape ordinary life, that I was living a more exciting life than people at home who got up every morning and went to work.

As time passed I realized that it's not only impossible to escape ordinary life, it's not necessary. The whole notion about needing to be somewhere else or someone else is what keeps us from realizing that we're already complete right here, right now. There's really nothing to achieve out there. Life doesn't have to entail great adventures though it doesn't have to exclude them either.

I first had the idea for this book four years ago when I returned to Denmark after reaching New York on my motorcycle. One evening I wrote down the table of contents for the book and even though I've since made some changes I've stuck to the original idea: to describe the qualities of effortlessness through the experiences of my motorcycle journey. However, what I thought "effortlessness" meant then and what I experience it to be now is very different. In fact, it's the opposite.

I believed that living effortlessly – to let the right action happen by itself – would work as a shield, protecting me from being hurt. If I was ridden of all hurt, *then* I would be free. I equated effortlessness with a life without pain and a life without pain with freedom.

I wanted to find an escape from unpleasant thoughts, emotions and feelings. I wanted a recipe for living in bliss – all the time. What's the point of letting the right action happen by itself if it doesn't protect me from hurt, rejection, feeling unworthy or wrong? None, I thought.

I now see that when I stop trying to cling to pleasure or escape pain in whatever form it takes, effortlessness is what remains. It's what's always the case. I'm free. Not free as a person but free as the aware presence to experience whatever life brings – both joy and sorrow. If freedom doesn't include the *possibility* of feeling sadness, anger or fear, is it real freedom? No. It's living in fear that "bad" stuff might happen to me. But if there's no escape from the "bad" stuff, if the "bad" stuff is allowed, what can then truly hurt me? Am I not free? Yes, indeed I am.

In this freedom the right action happens by itself because life doesn't have to be, look or even feel a certain way. Life includes *everything* – both "good" and "bad". This freedom is the birthplace of true compassion and connection. Life can unfold freely – for me and for others. I can experience life as the mystery it is. I can surrender the illusion of control and can enjoy the ride.

That is effortlessness.

Made in the USA
Lexington, KY
28 November 2013